Your Own
Wheeling to Healing

*A Guide to Healing Yourself and Groups
of People Who've Experienced
Adverse Childhood Experiences (ACEs)*

By Reverend James Encinas
Foreword by Linda Chamberlain, Ph.D.

Your Own Wheeling to Healing: A Guide to Healing Yourself and Groups of People Who've Experienced Adverse Childhood Experiences (ACEs)

Copyright © 2018 by James Encinas

Published by: www.new72publishing.com

Printed in the United States of America

ISBN # - paper 978-1-946054-12-8

ISBN # - ebook 978-1-946054-13-5

Library of Congress Number: 2018941132

Book cover design and interior formatting by Nelly Murariu

This book is a companion to *Wheeling to Healing…Broken Heart on a Bicycle: Understanding and Healing Adverse Childhood Experiences (ACEs)*©2017 by James Encinas.

All rights reserved. This book may not be reproduced in whole or in part, stored in a retrieval system, or transmitted in any form or by any means (electronic, mechanical, or other) without written permission from the publisher, except by a reviewer who may quote brief passages in a review.

Permissions

Grateful acknowledgment is made to Richard Rohr, OFM, and Patricia Mathes Cane, Ph.D. for permission to use a small amount of material of which they each hold a copyright.

Disclaimer

All content expressed or implied in this book is provided for information purposes only. The information is not intended to specify a means of diagnosing, treating, curing, or preventing cancer or any illness. It is not a substitute for treatment by a qualified medical or healthcare professional who should always be consulted before entering this program or any time the individual feels the need for assistance from a professional. Finally, the publisher, author, interviewees, doctors and healthcare practitioners referenced in this book expressly disclaim all responsibility for any liability, loss or risk, personal or otherwise, which is incurred as a consequence, directly or indirectly, of the use, effectiveness, safety or application of any of the procedures, treatments, therapies or recommendations mentioned, herein.

Contents

Foreword	5
Introduction	7
Creation of Safe Space	11
Brain Development and Function	21
Overview of the ACE Study	27
ACEs and Resilience	35
The Needs and Wants under the Feelings	43
The Power of Observation and Awareness of What's Hidden	49
Attachment Styles	55
You Are Not Your Traumas	63
Narrating the Future for Your Generations	67
Recognizing Loss and the Process of Grief	75
Kintsukuroi: To Repair by Using Gold	81
Change Is a Process, Not a One-Time Event	85
Heal, Healing, Healed	91
Nonviolence	97
Creativity as a Path to Self-Awareness	103
The Five C Words	111
Culture and Implicit Bias	115
Two Tasks, Two Masks	119
Creating a New Mask	125
Trauma and Theater	129
Role Play Mirror and True Self Mirror	135
You, and You in Relationship	139
Healing with Humor by Seeking Your Clown	143
Lights, Camera, Action, and… Shadow	147
Your Spiritual Truths	155
Past, Present, Hope, Healing	163

Foreword

Healing intergenerational trauma is within our reach because we understand the capacity of our brains to rewire, and the instinct of our bodies to heal, more than ever before. We also know that when adversity in childhood is left unaddressed and there are too few protective factors to provide resilience the child will experience an increased risk of perpetrating interpersonal violence as a youth and an adult.

Yet, many survivors of Adverse Childhood Experiences (ACEs) do not repeat the cycle. They overcome the residue of adversity, and they thrive. How can we grow resilience in ourselves and our communities, and, help more families, friends, and clients to make the healing journey?

James Encinas's companion guide to his book, *Wheeling to Healing…Broken Heart on a Bicycle: Understanding and Healing Adverse Childhood Experiences (ACES)* provides a toolbox to begin that healing journey and build resilience skills. There is no simple solution or cookie-cutter approach. For example, the story of Mani in "Creation of a Safe Space" describes the grinding reality of the potential transmission of trauma from generation to generation as we follow the tragic and preventable trajectory from traumatized child to adult perpetrator. However, even in the case of Mani, there were brief moments of awareness and connection that he was given to carry like a candle in his heart. That candle can keep burning to provide resilience, and, while we will never know, he may find times of emotional peace in his process of healing.

I first met James Encinas in a telephone conversation, and it was the first of many calls when we shared our stories, hopes, ideas, and visions for the future. We both believe that stories are powerful tools that bring people to a special place of understanding, sharing, and giving. As a scientist who is frequently spewing data, I know it is the stories that people connect with and remember. Stories have this amazing capacity to transcend our differences across cultures, genders, economics, and geography.

At the time James and I met, I was training and certifying in two different practices that use brain-body modalities to promote self-regulation, healing, and resilience. Understanding how self-regulation is compromised by memories of trauma, and how self-regulation skills are a gateway to healing, has become central to my work. Simple tools that help us to safely connect with physical and emotional sensations and regulate our internal systems can help survivors address how trauma and stress are stored in the body. In a recent series of reports on self-regulation and toxic stress, the Office of Planning, Research and Evaluation (OPRE; www.acf.hhs.gov/opre/research/project/toxic-stress-and-self-regulation-reports) recommends a self-regulation framework as a key strategy to help children and families overcome the impact of adversities.

James and I marvel at how, from classrooms to trauma support groups, there is often an expectation to sit for long periods of time without movement. Prolonged sitting is antithetical to everything we know about how the brain learns; it is also especially problematic for trauma survivors who frequently have difficulties with self-regulation. I shared with James the practices I was learning, particularly the work of Capacitar International (www.capacitar.org), and James integrated and adapted the mind-body-spirit exercises into the group sessions he led as part of a court-mandated education program for parolees. He would then send me his insights, ideas, and stories that were the greatest affirmation that I received in the new direction of my work.

Pat Cane, founder/executive director of Capacitar International, once said, "If someone reaches out to someone else to help them, they are on the road to recovery." I firmly believe that our *Wheeling to Healing* begins when we share our stories and it continues as we reach out to help, witness, and understand one another in healthier, better ways. Imagine if we, as a society, and in our own communities, could join hands in this journey.

I am grateful that James and I are on this road together. I hope you will find tools that you can use, adapt, and share with others as you help others to understand that it is never too late to engage in a process of healing.

Linda Chamberlain, Ph.D. MPH
Capacitar Facilitator, Founding Director of the Alaska Family Violence Prevention Project, Author, Speaker, and Educator

Introduction

Before my participation in the Aspen Teacher Fellowship 2011, I had not realized that the life I lived had meaning. That experience infused me with a sense of desire, responsibility, and the understanding that every human being is living on Earth for a purpose. Individual talents are to be used in service to both self and others. Although each individual's journey is unique, story is the glue that bonds one person to the next, and to the whole of humanity.

While at Aspen, I read Ursula Le Guin's short story, "The Ones Who Walk Away From Omelas." It is about an idyllic, magical place where all residents are happy. However, there is a secret in Omelas: a broom closet sized room with a locked door and no windows where a small child is locked inside. Le Guin described this child as unworthy.

I had once been that child.

The insights, tools, and exercises in this companion guide to *Wheeling to Healing—Broken Heart on a Bicycle: Understanding and Healing Adverse Childhood Experiences* are gifts I acquired while walking the path of my life's journey as an educator, author, speaker, and ordained minister. The experiences and emotions I had have taught me a very important lesson: Children and adults reflect the reality of the environments in which they were raised.

Recognition of this truth means that our societies must create new and different models and paradigms of healing to enhance wellbeing in individuals, families, and communities. Today, in every part of the world, millions of children are being raised in unpredictable and violent settings. Terror incubates and develops in their souls. The result is individuals who have a high probability of experiencing a life filled with spiritual, mental, and physical health disorders. Recognizing that "injury" and "hurt" are the first factors in undergoing the process of continual healing creates responsibility for individuals to understand these wounds.

I wrote *Your Own Wheeling to Healing: A Guide to Healing Yourself and Groups of People Who've Experienced Adverse Childhood Experiences (ACEs)* to provide a way to enable people searching for healing to meet all that will happen in their daily lives in healthy ways, and to maintain peace, honor and respect in all their relationships. The truth I see is that at the core of each person's essence is a relational being who is interrelated to all other humans, and who desires connection, support, witness, and love. The stories and concepts in both books can lead people to better understand healing—while in the act of healing—because it is a process that goes on for a lifetime.

There are many self-help books on the market today. While *Wheeling to Healing* has elements of my life story (from suffering domestic abuse in childhood to becoming a leader in promoting emotional healing for all), this companion guide is meant to support individuals, and communities of individuals, to undergo their own healing process—but I also know there is no formula to life. Life is completely dynamic!

An example of "dynamic" is in a scene from *Wheeling to Healing* in the moment I held a knife to my father's throat while saying, "Why couldn't you love me? Why couldn't you love me? Why couldn't you love me?" This companion book's mission is to build bridges between the frustration in feeling a lack of love to the joy and peace of feeling unconditional love.

On YouTube, the poet Maya Angelou speaks about this in a video titled: "Love is Freedom." As Jesus taught, "Love the Lord your God with all your heart and with all your soul and with all your mind and with all your strength and love your neighbor as yourself." Every person shares a need, want, and desire to be free to give and receive love. Such needs, wants, and desires give everyone a story-in-common. In sharing stories, without shame or guilt, it is possible to attain the kinds of love everyone seeks.

It is my intention that this book will find its way into the hands and hearts of individuals, families, teachers, community leaders, government workers, healing practitioners, social workers, mental health professionals, book clubs, social service groups, parenting classes, YMCA or YWCA classes, group homes, military communities, church groups, and people who make decisions throughout the criminal justice system. The stories, tools, and exercises provide good topics for silent thought or communal discussion.

While deep healing on the personal level is often recognized in private, interactive experiences benefit individual healing as well. Telling a story, and listening to the stories of others, allows narratives to exchange energy for the better via the power of words. The ability to share creates platforms to launch new skills and builds emotional resilience.

I believe in any effort that gives people opportunities to renew hope, and to get through their days in empowered, less needy, or less confused ways. To shine light on how to extend compassion to those lives fashioned by the effects of trauma is part of my intentions to bring healing to every individual. To end cycles of violence and trauma in families and communities, healing must be a focus. Healing occurs in the process of empowering and transforming individuals who have experienced trauma, especially during childhood.

While the need to heal is always present in someone who has experienced ACEs, the desire to heal can be complex, layered, and as difficult as was the pain that created the need. There is always the possibility of re-traumatization and need for great sensitivity by all who embark on the path towards healing.

Healing at the individual level expands to others in many unique ways.

Therefore, healing at the individual level must be addressed first.

Families and communities that are impacted by violence and trauma need to move beyond the current and narrow institutional focus of correcting behavior through harsh discipline and suppression of unpleasant emotions.

It is a truth that "Hurt people hurt people."

It is also a truth that "Healing people are healing people."

All human beings are capable of articulating their pain and suffering, asking for and finding relief, then making profound changes to prevent or minimize future hurts from happening. The right combination of self-exploration, reason, emotion, and experience is what leads to life-altering transformations. Providing individuals with tools for self-reflection, emotional self-regulation, the ability to regain balance, and to nurture personal growth through the "witness of others" who care, is what enables them to understand how past experiences influenced their development and shaped their present personal interactions with others.

When people are empowered to make sense of their personal narratives, to see and understand their capacity to make peace with others, to have meaningful and mutually rewarding relationships, a sustainable feeling of peace within is the result.

This is the feeling that every person needs, wants and desires.

The discussions that will arise because of this book afford individuals a safe space for processing their personal narrative, plus give them time for honest introspection and self-recognition. Used in a group setting, participants are enabled to collaborate with one another, validate others and themselves, re-educate, empower, and impart new positive relationships/relationship skills.

This type of work leads to ending the cycles of violence and trauma. In addition, it creates new cycles in which people are cognizant of healing, transforming, and empowering themselves and others to let their true purposes evolve. Be grounded in the profound belief that everyone has the power to give and receive love and understanding. Without understanding, there cannot be true love, and without love, there cannot be true understanding. The Earth is a place of duality—and when these kinds of beliefs are put into contrast, as they are here, the choice is easy to make.

Advances in the areas of neuroscience and brain development have provided new tools, explanations, and ways of dealing with troublesome or destructive behaviors. These approaches are grounded in the human body, in science, and in meaning. When one person understands their past, addresses the effects of trauma on memories and health, works to heal and find a new and ongoing love of self, they can achieve true compassion for others.

Readers are empowered to create and participate in unofficial communities of caring. As Jonathan Sacks wrote, "When we love and make loving commitments, we create families and communities within which people can grow and take risks, knowing that hands will be there to catch them should they fall." The ability of people to love themselves makes them able to love others…and makes each fall shorter, less traumatic, and easier to heal.

Creation of Safe Space

Start where you are. Use what you have. Do what you can.

~ ARTHUR ASHE ~

Aims and Intentions
* Creation of a place for safe communication
* Understanding self-regulation
* Mani's story

Tools and/or Exercises
* Talking circle
* Agreement and rules for a safe space
* Compassionate listening
* No Judgment. Just Love® pledge
* About Capacitar

Materials
* Large Post-it® tablet or poster board and Sharpie® marker
* No Judgment. Just Love® pledge from http://www.nojudgementjustlove.com/
* Capacitar's "Fingerholds" https://capacitar.org/
* Pens or pencils and paper or journals for note taking

Individuals in the process of healing must have spaces that are safe—devoid of shame and judgment. When a person can talk about the traumas they have experienced, be witnessed with compassion and without judgment, healing occurs.

In her book, *Creating Sanctuary: Toward the Evolution of Sane Societies,* Sandra L. Bloom, M.D. writes, "A corollary of the confusion between normality and health are our basic beliefs about deviance. Deviance is defined as 'departure from the accepted norm.'" Two examples of deviance are "sickness" and "badness." When people are "sick," they get more attention, and are excused from responsibility, until they are well. When people are "bad," they are held responsible for their behaviors and actions, which leads to justification for punishment. When "bad" behavior is witnessed, observers ask, "What is wrong with you?" which can provide fuel for even more "bad" behavior.

Much of what is judged as sickness and/or badness is a direct or indirect result of "injury." Often, the injury was inflicted during youth, a time when there is a universal expectation that a caretaker is responsible for the physical health and emotional wellbeing of the child. The idea of "injury" is a social problem—and it is greater than the problems of a "sick" or "bad" individual.

Although you can never presume to fully understand what it's like to walk in another's shoes, it is important to ask the question, "What happened to them?" instead of, "What's wrong with them?" The English philosopher John Locke, whose ideas influenced the foundation of democracy, knew and understood this. Locke believed babies are born with what he called an "empty" mind, a tabula rasa. The tabula rasa is shaped by experience, sensations, and reflection, and it is at the root of what the ACE study brought to light. People are not born violent or evil; they are taught and learn to hate, and they act on that hate.

To prevent judgments about "injury," "sick," and "bad," healing in groups must create safe spaces in which to meet and talk. A safe space is to be defined by the group, and rules are discussed, agreed upon, and used at every meeting.

Because individual life-experience stories connect and unify people through the action of compassionate, nonjudgmental witness, this guide offers a window into the lives of certain people with whom I developed a relationship in the course of my work. Their stories illustrate how people are shaped by both traumatic and beneficial experiences in childhood that remain until the end of life, and why it is important that they be shared in a safe space.

Here, Mani's story is provided for two reasons. The first is to show the importance of maintaining a safe and stable environment with clear boundaries.

And second, to demonstrate the reality of what happens in groups that meet for the purpose of healing is that people want to "save" or "fix" others as much as they want to be "saved" or "fixed." The story of Mani demonstrates that the only person who can "save" or "fix" or give the grace of healing is that single individual's own self.

When I was facilitating a court mandated, 52-week program to individuals who had been convicted of domestic violence, we met in the Valley Family Center in the San Fernando area. The room I was assigned to for those meetings was designed as a classroom. We sat in a circle, created trust, and built community.

Mani's Story

Mani was a physically imposing man. He had spent a lot of time pumping iron and building a protective wall of muscle. A man who had been deeply and consistently hurt, he did not know how to behave without hurting others or himself.

From the moment he entered our group, Mani expressed a tremendous need to share the traumatic experience of his arrest. Helicopters flying overhead, a SWAT team kicking down the front door, men with shotguns drawn, throwing him face first onto the ground, handcuffing him, violently dragging him through the yard, his feelings of shame, humiliation, and helpless rage washing over him as neighbors watched him being thrown into the police car and driven away. He couldn't and didn't understand why he had to go through that trauma just for throwing a small glass of water at his wife.

Over the next two months, as we worked together in a group, Mani shared more bits and pieces of his life. For years, he struggled with feelings of depression and hopelessness. He had been in and out of prison as an adult, and had been physically abused at the hands of his father.

One of the stories he told to demonstrate his fearlessness in the face of death occurred when he was 10. He was already carrying a gun and working for a drug cartel in his home state of Sinaloa, Mexico. One of his bosses thought Mani was stealing and put a gun to his face. Mani said he just stared at the man and said, "Go ahead. Pull the trigger." He told us that he "wasn't afraid to die."

The times he was most animated were when he was telling us about his kids, especially his little girl who was born with Down syndrome. She was often the only one who could break up the fights he had with his wife because she would walk over to him and hold his hand. One day he stopped in with his daughter to tell us he couldn't attend the group because he couldn't find a babysitter.

Mani was often frustrated. He felt that people didn't understand him, specifically his wife. She was the only adult he felt ever loved him, other than his mother. During his second suicide attempt, he experienced a feeling and witnessed a place that he couldn't really describe, but he felt happy there, and was surrounded by a beautiful bright light. Then, his mother, who died when he was six, appeared, and he also saw others who had died. God and his mother told him it was not his time to join them. When he woke up, his wife was sitting on his hospital bed, holding his hand.

On one particularly stressful day, Mani's rage and unmet needs hit a tipping point and he blew his lid while in our group. When confronted with the fact that the words he was using to describe his wife were demeaning and derogatory, Mani got very angry and defensive. He demanded to know why I was picking on him. Angry that I asked him to leave the room, he refused. After repeating the request a couple more times, I could see his anger was escalating. I told Mani that for the health and safety of the group, if he did not leave, the police would be called.

When the police arrived, they tried to talk to Mani. However, he was just too aroused and angry. When they informed him that if he did not leave he was going to face arrest, Mani laughed nervously but continued to be non-compliant. Three officers were in the room and when one of them put an arm on his shoulder in an attempt to guide him towards the door Mani tensed up, asked not to be touched and said, "You wouldn't like it if I touched your gun." Their response was immediate. Mani was forcibly handcuffed, escorted outside, and placed into a patrol car.

I wish I could say that through our work together Mani acquired the tools and skills to make healthier choices; but I feel sad that I cannot. The system, his life, and his everyday struggles have been too much for him. Mani lives in a perpetual hyper-alert state, constantly in fight-or-flight mode, in a chronic physiological stress response. His inability to acquire a good job is due to his felony conviction, a lack of healthy communication skills, and the inability to self-regulate. This hyper-vigilant man is filled with a seething fury that he carries wherever he goes.

The example Mani's story sets is the reason a meeting space must be safe.

Talking Circle

When the tools and exercises in this guide are used to facilitate groups, the best seating plan is the one used for talking circles, peacemaking circles, or healing circles. This model is from the traditions of indigenous people who knew that sitting in circles to consider solutions or discuss answers to questions and/or problems was an efficient and good way to create community.

The talking circle model for use in your own *Wheeling to Healing* fosters deep listening and reflection in conversation and provides a safe environment for people who are committed to helping one another in healing. People who sit in circles are less prone to confrontation and anger. The circle creates a feeling of unity.

Once the room has been arranged where all members are in a circle, the facilitator holds an object to be used as the "talking stick" and opens discussion with a prayer, poem or spiritual reading. A discussion on the elements needed for group safety follows as the "talking stick" moves clockwise around the circle, for each person to speak. Everyone else will remain quiet. The circle is complete when everyone has contributed their thoughts around what they need to be comfortable and feel safe while expressing themselves.

Agreement on Rules for a Safe Meeting Space

During the first talking circle exercise, the goal is to create rules for group safety. The facilitator of the talking circle will write each person's ideas for what is necessary for them to feel safe. It is best to use a large Post-it® paper, poster board or white board to capture comments. After everyone has identified the safe space elements, time must be allowed for group discussion to tweak, solidify, or expand on the list. Anyone who has something to say regarding the process is given the opportunity to speak. Once there is group consensus, the final list of rules should be copied onto a blank poster board or a large Post-it® paper.

Compassionate Listening

The group facilitator asks for a volunteer from the talking circle to assist with modeling compassionate listening. The facilitator and volunteer take chairs into the center of the group, face each other, and sit down. The two sit tall, yet relaxed, look at each other in the eyes and take a few deep breaths. This will help them stay calm. Once the two are focused, calm, and present, the volunteer asks the facilitator:

- Why did you come to this group?
- What are some words that describe your relationship with your partner or your closest loved one?

- What are some words that describe your relationship with your parents or children?
- What do you want to learn here?

When the facilitator has answered the questions, it is the volunteer's turn to answer. After modeling this exercise, have the group create pairs—one as a speaker, one as a listener—to spend five minutes in each role. Depending on the size of the group, the participants can rotate to other partners. This will give the group a chance to participate with one another in the act of compassionate listening for the four questions presented.

Next, ask each person to choose a different partner and engage in compassionate listening with different questions:

- How do you define yourself? Start with "I am..." or "I come from..."
- What matters most to you? Start with "I honor..." or "I love..."
- What do you think the people you love remember about you when you are not with them?

Once each person participates in each role, the facilitator invites everyone back to the talking circle and encourages the sharing of thoughts on the 'pair share' experience. Give support to those who may be feeling uncomfortable about sharing their experience in front of a group. Using compassionate listening builds relationships among the group members.

No Judgment. Just Love®

Compassionate listening means to listen intently while suspending judgment of what a person says in speech as well as what they communicate nonverbally. After the compassionate listening exercise, give an opportunity to participate in the movement known as No Judgment. Just Love®. ShaRon Rea, author and family relationships coach, came up with a vision for what the world looks like when people treat one another with love in place of judgment. Here is the pledge she created:

> Take the Pledge for No Judgment. Just Love.®
>
> It's Time.
>
> Imagine a world filled with people who treat each other with respect and allowance…because of you.
>
> Make personal commitment to live the message of No Judgment. Just Love.® By moving away from divisive thoughts and actions. Join us and sign the Pledge. Motivate yourself and inspire others to live together in peace, with respect for different beliefs and opinions. Everyone is valuable and deserves love without judgment, including you.

***

I Pledge…

To be kind and loving to myself so I can show kindness and love to others.

To recognize when I'm in divisive judgment mode, pause and change to something better.

To be diplomatic, gentle and speak positive words.

To be innovative by asking different questions and listening for new answers.

To allow people the freedom to be themselves.

To know I don't have to understand everyone. I can just allow and let them be.

To be the joyful expression of forgiveness and let things go.

To look for and find more things to be grateful for in my life.

To include fun and laughter in every day.

To seek, find, engage in and promote international friendships.

To appreciate nature and treat the Earth, our planet, well.

To live in ways that inspire others to live with No Judgment. Just Love.®

Signed _____ Date _____

About Capacitar

The nonprofit Capacitar "is an international network of solidarity and empowerment working in over 40 countries in the Americas, Africa, Europe, the Middle East and Asia, and it is committed to communities affected by violence, poverty and trauma." Their "mission is to heal ourselves and heal our world. We teach simple holistic wellness practices that help people tap into the wisdom of their own body, mind, and spirit. This leads to healing, wholeness and peace in the individual and in the world."

According to Bruce Perry M.D., Ph.D., the founder of the Child Trauma Academy, repetition is key to the development of the human brain. Repetition leads to mastery, which increases confidence and builds self-esteem. Willpower, self-control, and self-regulation may be built into a person's operating system through repetition.

Patricia Mathes Cane, Ph.D., created the "Emergency Response Tool Kit" (www.capacitar.org/wp-content/uploads/EngCapEmergKit.pdf) for Capacitar. The tool, "Fingerholds" is an excellent way to engage the use of repetition for the practice of self-regulation.

Dr. Cane believes that, "health of body, mind and emotions is continuously affected by trauma, violence, weather, diet, environment, daily news and the challenges of life." She identified simple, ancient, healing skills that empower people to live with peace and wellbeing, no matter what is happening in their lives. These tools are for any person—survivors of trauma, caregivers of children, the infirm, the elderly, or persons overwhelmed and stressed by daily life. The challenge is to build these practices into a lifestyle so they become second nature and can be readily called upon whenever a person becomes aware of traumatic stress, energy drain, depressed feelings, or loss of center.

"Fingerholds"

The "fingerholds" tool is helpful to use in daily life. In difficult or challenging situations when tears, anger, or anxiety arise, the fingers are held to bring peace, focus and calm so that the appropriate response or action may be taken. The fingerholds practice may also be done for relaxation with music, or used before going to sleep to release the problems of the day and bring deep peace to body and mind.

While referring to the illustration, discuss information on the fingers and their corresponding emotions:

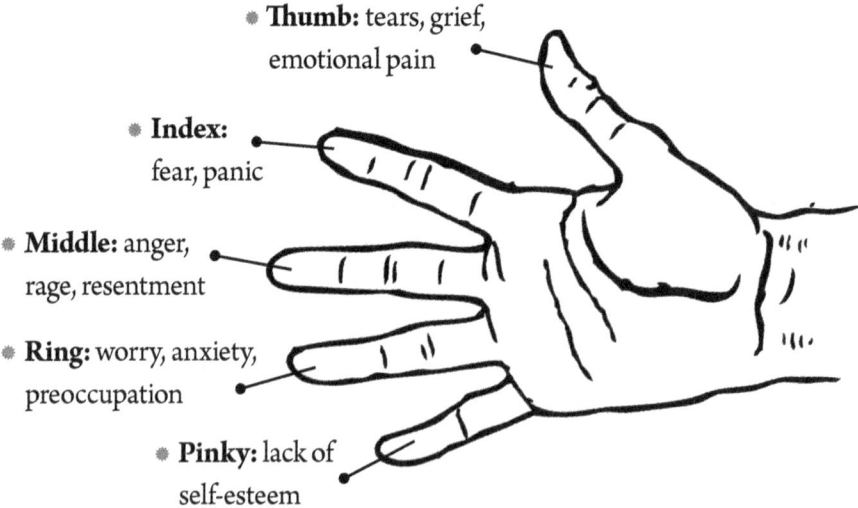

- **Thumb:** tears, grief, emotional pain
- **Index:** fear, panic
- **Middle:** anger, rage, resentment
- **Ring:** worry, anxiety, preoccupation
- **Pinky:** lack of self-esteem

Ask each person to hold their right thumb with their left hand, then read aloud from the document instructions for breathing through the emotional responses related to the thumb. Repeat for the four fingers. Spend two to five minutes on each finger.

Brain Development and Function

Everything we do, every thought we've ever had, is produced by the human brain. But exactly how it operates remains one of the biggest unsolved mysteries, and it seems the more we probe its secrets, the more surprises we find.

~ NEIL DEGRASSE TYSON ~

Aims and Intentions
- The human brain and its functions
- Ann's story
- Appreciate the healing value of writing or drawing in a journal

Tools and/or Exercises
- Watch a video by Bruce Perry, M.D., Ph.D., titled "State Dependent Functioning"
- Watch a video by Dan Siegel, M.D. showing how to model the brain with your fist
- Words and/or images exercise on brain function
- Mindfulness through guided meditation

Materials
- Computer and A/V equipment
- Video by Bruce Perry, M.D., Ph.D. www.youtube.com/watch?v=1uCn7VX6BPQ
- Video by Dan Siegel, M.D. www.youtube.com/watch?v=gm9CIJ74Oxw

- Pens or pencils and paper or journals
- Large Post-it® tablet and Sharpie® marker

Adverse Childhood Experiences do not discriminate. Many of the men and women I've worked with in groups live at the intersection of poverty and violence. Everyone's ACEs affect all of us, without regard to social class, gender identity, sexual orientation, race, or any physical, emotional or intellectual abilities/disabilities.

Advances in neuroscience and research point to a strong relationship between childhood exposure to abuse and trauma and lifelong negative health outcomes. Understanding how traumas experienced by young brains impact human development gives life context, meaning, hope, and opens all kinds of opportunities for healing.

The Human Brain

The brain, a relational organ, performs best when it receives proper nurturing so that brain cells connect, communicate, and process all functions in the most effective way. Brain growth and development depends on what it perceives and how it is used at every age—from fetus to senior citizen. When all parts of the brain are working together, the concept of an "integrated nervous system" is possible, and it's necessary to understand.

Knowledge of the brain and how it works is necessary for every class participant who has experienced ACEs. The participants must be able to contextualize how their brain responds because of the trauma they experienced—as far back as pre-birth. The best way to explain the brain's role in the human's "integrated nervous system" is through a 10:41-minute video titled, "State Dependent Functioning." Dr. Bruce Perry who is an expert on brain function narrates it. He is both a medical doctor and a psychiatrist. Here is the link to the video: www.youtube.com/watch?v=1uCn7VX6BPQ. After watching, allow time for a group discussion.

Next, watch Dan Siegel, M.D. demonstrate brain modeling with the human hand in a 2:31 minute video at www.youtube.com/watch?v=gm9CIJ74Oxw. Allow time for more discussion and "modeling" after watching the video.

Ann's Story

In the beginning, Ann was guarded and reluctant to share or make personal self-disclosures. As her sense of safety in the group developed, she went beyond sharing only information about her relationship with her daughter. After a first marriage at age 17 to an abusive spouse who she left when she was eight months pregnant, Ann had been arrested for physically assaulting her second husband. On the morning she walked away from her first husband, Ann swore she would never let another man mistreat her. Little did she know that the hurt she experienced would one day cause her to hurt another.

While in the group, it was both the ACE Study information and brain development lessons that sparked Ann's interest in healing. Her light went on, and her floodgates opened as she shared guilt, concern, and hatred as well as love for her own abusive mother. A devout woman of faith, Ann felt conflicted.

In a confidential conversation apart from our group, Ann said she had been diagnosed with a mental health problem and that the ACE's information and brain knowledge she was acquiring was giving her hope. She now had the courage to engage healing for herself, and be a better mother to her daughter. Ann didn't want her daughter to experience the childhood she had experienced. When she learned about the impacts of domestic violence on a fetus during pregnancy, rather than making Ann feel hopeless, it gave her hope. It gave her new insight and a better perspective into her daughter's academic struggles, and the ability to better support her child's growth and development.

Ann became a leader and role model for many of the women in that group. Embracing everyone with an encouraging and open heart, she inspired and motivated us. Her courage, empathy, and compassion changed us for the better.

Words and/or Images on Brain Function

The act of writing thoughts or drawing images in a journal is taking action to slow down and express thoughts. This kind of action is where emotional healing can take root and grow if keeping a journal for writing and/or drawing is done as a regular practice.

Hand out pens and blank sheets of paper to each participant. Ask them to think about what they've just learned about brain function. Allow five to fifteen minutes for writing or drawing something they found useful. Ask about a time when they experienced a joyous situation that created a good connection; or a miserable situation that caused disconnection in their brain, and how they'd deal with it now, knowing what they've just learned.

As the class spends time writing or drawing, the facilitator can write out on a whiteboard, Post-it® large sheet or simply verbally ask the following questions:

- What do you want to explore through today's opportunity to write or draw?
- What thoughts are going through your mind about a recent experience?
- Are you aware of your breathing, of your body, how are you feeling?

When the time for this type of expression ends, allow those who want the opportunity to share what they've written or drawn to do so.

Mindfulness through Guided Meditation

After the writing/drawing exercise and sharing, ask class members to sit in a comfortable position. The facilitator leads the guided meditation by asking them to close their eyes and take three deep breaths. Once they are focused and relaxed, read this text aloud:

> *See yourself in a place, real or imaginary, where you feel safe, peaceful, and calm. Take your time to be in this place with all your senses. Is it warm or cool? Make yourself comfortable. Are you standing, sitting, or lying on your back? Do you sense any smells or sounds?*
>
> *Let your breathing deepen. Allow yourself to increase your feelings of relaxation with every in-breath and every out-breath. Experience your breath gradually filling up your entire body.*
>
> *Imagine this relaxing energy moving through your body in waves, reaching every part of you.*
>
> *We will have some silence now, for this feeling to take hold.*
>
> ***
>
> *Wherever you find yourself—at a seashore on a beautiful day or home in your favorite chair—it's the perfect time of day, the perfect time of year, for you to be there.*
>
> *Let yourself explore what it feels like—temperature, air circulation, textures, a close-in view, a landscape, smells, sounds, tastes—anything else that is sensed or felt.*
>
> *A bit more silence now, to allow expansion of details.*
>
> ***

> *Anytime you need to, you can now go to this special place. It will always be there for you, and the more you visit it the easier it will be to access in your imagination.*

Gradually bring their attention back to their breath, from deep and slow to the normal pattern of awareness. Tell them that it's time to return to the class and when ready they can begin to bring their focus back to the room. Tell them to become aware of their bodies in their chairs, the soles of their feet on the ground, their hands. Ask them to be aware of any sense of tension or relaxation in their muscles. When they are all 'back' from the meditation, let them know that short meditations can be practiced in just a few minutes as needed throughout the day. It is an easy and powerful way to calm and regulate your nervous system.

Overview of the ACE Study

I spent my childhood in an imaginary world—probably because I needed an escape. I think that's one of the reasons people have imaginations—because they can't maintain existence here.

~ RICKIE LEE JONES ~

Aims and Intentions
* ACEs and their impact on personal development
* David's story

Tools and/or Exercises
* ACEs overview discussion: "Gold into Lead"
* ACE assessment tool
* Words and/or images about your childhood
* Compassionate listening—sharing stories from childhood

Materials
* Video about toxic stress: www.youtube.com/watch?v=rVwFkcOZHJw
* Individual ACE assessment link: http://www.acesconnection.com/g/san-diego-county-aces-connection-group/clip/aces-and-the-unified-science-of-human-development-jane-stevens-30-minutes-ppt-pptx
* Pens or pencils and paper or journals
* Post-it® large tablet and Sharpie® marker

The following is an excerpt from an article written by Jane Ellen Stevens, ACEsTooHigh News, October 3, 2012: "The Adverse Childhood Experiences

Study—the largest, most important public health study you never heard of—began in an obesity clinic."

"Children with toxic stress live much of their lives in fight, flight or fright (freeze) mode. They respond to the world as a place of constant danger. With their brains overloaded with stress hormones and unable to function appropriately, they cannot focus on learning. In school, they tend to fall behind or fail to develop healthy relationships with peers or create problems with teachers and principals because they are unable to trust adults. Some kids do all three. With despair, guilt, and frustration pecking away at their psyches, they often find solace in food, alcohol, tobacco, methamphetamines, inappropriate sex, high-risk sports, and/or work and over-achievement. They don't regard these coping methods as problems. Consciously or unconsciously, they use them as solutions to escape from depression, anxiety, anger, fear and shame."

ACEs and Their Impact on Personal Development

It is important to gain an understanding of the impact of trauma on personal development and to learn that when one faces chronic and unpredictable stressors, the developing body and brain are flooded with stress chemicals that inflame cells. Stress (and its side effects) alters the expression of genes that control hormone output. This creates an overactive and inflammatory stress response pattern. The brakes that should turn that stress response off are worn out and stop working properly. This breakdown leads to emotional floods of anger or anxiety that interfere with clear thinking and self-control. The inflammation that occurs gets in the way of proper synapse formation in the brain.

Exposure to repeated traumas, and the stress that results, creates bad memories in every cell of the body. As trauma is 'dialed in' to a person's brain and body, it is difficult to 'dial it out.' Each experience of stress builds on itself, and each episode interferes with the ability to think in a calm, clear way. Lack of self-control then becomes a pattern…and a problem…as it did in the life story of David.

David's Story

David was reared by a single mother who struggled to make ends meet and did not have the time or tools to give him the attention and guidance he required. From that space of inattention, and because his mother's boyfriend was an abusive alcoholic, he lost his way.

His school experience mirrored David's home experience. The neighborhood he lived in was unsafe and the school environment was too. Feeling angry, hurt, and neglected, David was often in trouble. When fights broke out in the schoolyard David was usually right there along with the other angry and hurt boys.

By the age of 12, with nowhere else to turn, David sought safety and protection in a gang. The gang gave him attention, love, and care in the moment. What he didn't know was that gang membership is long-term, and it included the pitfalls that hanging out with the wrong crowd brings. At age 15, David encountered the juvenile justice system.

He and some gang members went to buy beer, but did not have enough money and stole what they couldn't afford. A clerk in the store tried to stop the group, but grabbed David. He panicked and hit the clerk in the head with a bottle of beer. The assault led to two years of life in a juvenile detention center.

David's life story illustrates several Adverse Childhood Experiences as they are listed on the ACE assessment tool. He was a victim of toxic stress in childhood. Here is a short (1.51-minute) video, www.youtube.com/watch?v=rVwFkcOZHJw from the Center on the Developing Child at Harvard University titled "Toxic Stress Derails Healthy Development."

ACEs Overview Discussion: "Gold into Lead"

The title of the journal article about the ACE Study contained the phrase "Turning Gold into Lead." The alchemists of old worked on finding a magic formula to turn lead into gold—something ugly and common into something beautiful and valuable. The reverse—turning something beautiful and valuable into something ugly and common—is what often happens to a human being who is the equivalent of "gold" at birth, but who turns to "lead" after being subjected to traumas.

Healing, and change for the better, is more than identifying a problem and applying a new technique, solution, balm, or pill. True healing and good change requires listening to your inner wisdom. When you engage healing on the spirit level, you reconnect with your light and transform.

This is the time for a presentation regarding the ACE Study. Here is a link with a download to more useful information before you use the ACE Assessment tool: http://www.acesconnection.com/g/san-diego-county-aces-connection-group/clip/aces-and-the-unified-science-of-human-development-jane-stevens-30-minutes-ppt-pptx.

Individual ACE Assessment

Prior to your 18th birthday:

1. Did a parent or other adult in the household often or very often:

...swear at you, insult you, put you down, or humiliate you?

...act in a way that made you afraid that you might be physically hurt?

Yes ☐   No ☐

2. Did a parent or other adult in the household often or very often:

...push, grab, slap, or throw something at you?

...ever hit you so hard that you had marks or were injured?

Yes ☐   No ☐

3. Did an adult or person at least five years older than you ever:

...touch or fondle you in a sexual way?

...have you touch their body in a sexual way?

...attempt or actually have oral, anal or vaginal intercourse with you?

Yes ☐   No ☐

4. Did you often or very often feel that:

...no one in your family loved you or thought you were important or special?

...your family didn't look out for each other, feel close, or support each other?

Yes ☐   No ☐

5. Did you often or very often feel that:

...you didn't have enough to eat?

...had to wear dirty clothes?

...had no one to protect you?

...your parents were too drunk or high to take care of you?

Yes ☐   No ☐

6. Were your parents separated or divorced?

Yes ☐   No ☐

7. Was your mother or stepmother:

...often, or very often, pushed, grabbed, slapped, or had something thrown at her?

...often, or very often, kicked, bitten, hit with a fist, or hit with something hard?

...hit or threatened with a gun or knife?

Yes ☐   No ☐

8. Did you live with anyone who was a problem drinker or alcoholic, or who used street drugs?

Yes ☐   No ☐

9. Was a household member depressed or mentally ill, or attempt suicide?

Yes ☐   No ☐

10.   Did a household member go to prison?

Yes ☐   No ☐

Now add up your "Yes" answers. This is your ACE score. _____ / 10

Words and/or Images about Your Childhood

Once everyone has their ACE scores, spend 15-20 minutes writing or drawing more specific responses to the questions about childhood.

To expand into group discussion after the ACE assessment and journaling session, allow members to engage in compassionate listening and share stories based on these questions:

1. Where did you grow up?
2. How did you know your parents or caretakers loved you?
3. Did anyone ever say, "I love you"?
4. How did your parents or caretakers show or express their love to you and to one another?
5. What were qualities you liked about yourself when you were a child?
6. Who were the important people in your life?
7. Did you have experiences of lack? Of need? Of want? Of loss? If so, describe one or all.
8. Did you feel important in your family?
9. Were you fearful as a child?
10. If you could give advice now to the child you were, what would you say?

ACEs and Resilience

We live in a time when science is validating what humans have known throughout the ages: that compassion is not a luxury; it is a necessity for our well-being, resilience, and survival.

~ JOAN HALIFAX ~

Aims and Intentions
- Compare ACEs to resilience
- Reina's Story

Tools and/or Exercises
- Group discussion about trauma and resilience
- ACE Resilience assessment
- Three steps to foster resiliency
- Tree of Life drawing exercise
- Compassionate listening

Materials
- Individual Resilience Assessment and pencils
- Colored pencils, markers or crayons and sheets of white drawing paper
- Post-it® large tablet and Sharpie® marker

The counterbalance to trauma is resilience. Resilience is the ability of an individual or community to withstand and rebound from stress. There is a large and growing body of research on the resiliency factors for individuals and groups. Researchers have made a paradigm shift away from studying what is "wrong" with "problem" students to the study of what is "right" with them. (Some people refer to this as a shift to the "strength model" from the "deficit model.") Resiliency research is the study of how some students, despite the stressors in their lives, manage to adapt, and in some cases, thrive. The majority of these studies reveal that resiliency is a process, and a combination of individual and environmental factors.

Traumas endured during childhood can be measured. But, traumas can be balanced by or neutralized with experiences that make a person feel safe, calm, valued, and loved. The story Reina tells is an example of how she met and used her reserve of resilience.

Reina's Story

Reina didn't go very far in school because she got pregnant at an early age. Two years later, Reina gave birth to a boy she named Jesus. At that time, her parents said she could continue to live with them, but she was going to have to earn her keep.

Living in a poor, rural community in Mexico, Reina found a job at a sweatshop sewing buttons on shirts. She barely made enough money to feed and clothe herself and her sons, even though she worked 12 to 14 hours a day. Working long hours, while also being a mother and a daughter, Reina longed for a moment of leisure when she might go dancing, but there was no such opportunity.

Reina's mother ran a truck stop type of restaurant from the house, and Reina often thought about hiding in a truck and running away from her life. However, she knew she could never desert her family, especially her sons.

One of the most popular dishes her mother made for the truckers was soft-boiled sea turtle eggs. The tops of the shells were cut and the egg was topped with a pinch of salt or fresh salsa. Although illegal, these eggs were thought to be an aphrodisiac.

Reina thought of the local fishermen she knew and decided to ask them if she could buy the eggs they gathered. Then she visited other restaurants nearby to ask if they would buy the prepared eggs from her.

She then made a deal with some of the truckers who ate at her house to help her deliver the eggs to the restaurants. Reina knew her plan was risky and illegal but she was at a point in her life that it was a risk she was willing to take.

For a number of years Reina made a good living selling the prepared turtle eggs. But someone in her village informed the police, who jailed her. She managed to call her older son, who knew where Reina hid the money she made, and had him bring it to her so she could pay off the police.

The week she was jailed and released, a friend of hers returned from the United States for a visit. Reina had given this friend the money to pay coyote smugglers to get them across the border. The friend told Reina her entrepreneurial spirit would do very well in the land of opportunity, where there were safe and legal pathways to providing for her and her sons. So, Reina packed her things and asked her mother to care for Jesus while she and her first-born settled. A year later Reina returned to her village to retrieve Jesus and she again crossed the desert to realize her dream of an easier life.

Reina's story demonstrates physical, emotional, intellectual, and spiritual resilience.

Group Discussion about Trauma and Resilience

It is amazing how people withstand multiple childhood traumas to get back up with a fighting spirit. People always have the choice to stay 'broken.' The ones who choose to rise with their resilience and work hard as individuals are always able to transform their situations for the better.

Here, according to www.merriam-webster.com, is resilience defined: "resilience: noun re·sil·ience \ ri-zil-yən(t)s \, 1: the capability of a strained body to recover its size and shape after deformation caused especially by compressive stress; 2: an ability to recover from or adjust easily to misfortune or change."

When one experiences childhood adversity, behavior control (and the ability to make good choices) is compromised over the course of a lifetime. A traumatized person may have poor impulse control, self-destructive behavior, aggression issues, sleep disturbances, eating disorders, substance abuse, excessive compliance and difficulty understanding and complying with the reasonable rules that keep societies from running amok.

Traumas suffered in childhood are reduced when love and care from another person is experienced and positive relationships are built. The relationship can come from a family member, a friend, an acquaintance or a stranger. It can take the form of someone being there when you most need them to say the word or words you most want and need to hear, or to hear the words you need and want to say. It can be enough that they are just present for you as a silent, nonjudgmental, loving witness of your being.

Use Reina's story to allow group conversation. Discuss the definition of resilience as given by the dictionary, and in examples from real life.

After time spent in discussion about resilience, move into the individual measurement of resilience by using the assessment tool.

The ACE Resilience Assessment

Please circle the most accurate answer under each statement:

1. **I believe that my mother loved me when I was little.**
   Definitely True | Probably True | Not Sure | Probably Not True | Definitely Not True

2. **I believe that my father loved me when I was little.**
   Definitely True | Probably True | Not Sure | Probably Not True | Definitely Not True

3. **When I was little, other people helped my mother and father take care of me and they seemed to love me.**
   Definitely True | Probably True | Not Sure | Probably Not True | Definitely Not True

4. I've heard that when I was an infant someone in my family enjoyed playing with me, and I enjoyed it, too.
   Definitely True | Probably True | Not Sure | Probably Not True | Definitely Not True

5. When I was a child, there were relatives in my family who made me feel better if I was sad or worried.
   Definitely True | Probably True | Not Sure | Probably Not True | Definitely Not True

6. When I was a child, neighbors or my friends' parents seemed to like me.
   Definitely True | Probably True | Not Sure | Probably Not True | Definitely Not True

7. When I was a child, teachers, coaches, youth leaders or ministers were there to help me.
   Definitely True | Probably True | Not Sure | Probably Not True | Definitely Not True

8. Someone in my family cared about how I was doing in school.
   Definitely True | Probably True | Not Sure | Probably Not True | Definitely Not True

9. My family, neighbors and friends talked often about making our lives better.
   Definitely True | Probably True | Not Sure | Probably Not True | Definitely Not True

10. We had rules in our house and were expected to keep them.
    Definitely True | Probably True | Not Sure | Probably Not True | Definitely Not True

11. When I felt really bad, I could almost always find someone I trusted to talk to.
    Definitely True | Probably True | Not Sure | Probably Not True | Definitely Not True

12. As a youth, people noticed that I was capable and could get things done.
    Definitely True | Probably True | Not Sure | Probably Not True | Definitely Not True

13. I was independent and a go-getter.
    Definitely True | Probably True | Not Sure | Probably Not True | Definitely Not True

14. I believed that life is what you make it.
    Definitely True | Probably True | Not Sure | Probably Not True | Definitely Not True

Of these 14 protective factors, how many did you circle as "Definitely True" or "Probably True"? _____ Of those circled, how many are still true for you today? _____

Three Steps to Foster Resiliency

1. To foster resiliency and hope, provide unconditional love in a safe and caring environment.

2. Always empower, never disempower. In other words, be assertive in addressing inappropriate conduct; however, avoid any controlling method that might resemble the behavior of individuals who have learned to use violence in order to cope/survive.

3. Allow for individuals who have built some resiliency to help themselves by helping others. Watch as this occurs organically. As members of the group bond, they develop empathy and compassion for the welfare of others and want to offer support by helping others deal with common challenges.

Tree of Life Drawing

Ask the group to break into groups of up to four people. Provide each group with some colored pencils, markers or crayons and one sheet of paper per person. Each team member's task is to draw a complete tree. The tree must include its root system, trunk, branches, leaves, buds, fruit, flowers, and thorns.

While the class members are doing this, prepare a Post-it® tablet page with the following information:

- **Roots** = life influences and beliefs (positive and negative)
- **Trunk** = life structure and personal aspects that are firm or fixed
- **Branches** = relationships and connections, directions, interests, how time is spent
- **Leaves** = information and knowledge and sources thereof
- **Buds** = ideas and hopes for the future; their own potential
- **Fruit** = achievements
- **Flowers** = what makes them special; their strengths
- **Thorns** = challenges, threats and difficulties

Compassionate Listening

When the class members have completed their drawings, have the group come together and share what they've learned about themselves from comparing their drawing of the tree to the corresponding meaning of each part (as listed on the poster).

After all have spoken, lead another group discussion on how the ages, stages, personal and family histories, and community context at each phase or time in an individual's life matters for obtaining, building and having the capacity for resilience. Talk about why being resilient means asking for help and revealing one's vulnerability.

The Needs and Wants under the Feelings

*Emotional intelligence is the ability to perceive emotions,
to access and generate emotions so as to assist thought,
to understand emotions and emotional knowledge,
and to reflectively regulate emotions so as
to promote emotional and intellectual growth.*

~ MAYER & SALOVEY, 1997 ~

Aims and Intentions
- Understanding Maslow's "Hierarchy of Needs"
- Brandon's story

Tools and/or Exercises
- "OF NEEDS"
- Role play exercise
- The emotional impact of flowers
- Words and/or images exercise about anger

Materials
- Link to Maslow's "Hierarchy of Needs"
  https://www.simplypsychology.org/maslow.html
- "OF NEEDS" information: http://www.echoparenting.org/wp-content/uploads/2012/04/week5_Ofneeds.pdf

- Link to use of flowers:
  http://www.growerdirect.com/emotional-impact-of-flowers
- Pens or pencils and paper or journals
- Fresh flowers (a bloom for each class member)

Abraham Maslow's "Hierarchy of Needs" (https://www.simplypsychology.org/maslow.html) was first published in 1943. His concept of need is often illustrated as a triangle: At the base are the physical needs like food, water, sleep, and health. Above those basics are needs for safety and shelter. Once those needs are met comes a need to receive and give love, and to feel a sense of belonging. These needs, when all are fulfilled, give rise to a need for self-esteem (including esteem felt for others) and finally a need to know and appreciate the self—or self-actualization, awareness of one's own personal power and ability to appreciate and use freedom in appropriate ways.

These needs are either met or unmet—when unmet, they become wants. The story of Brandon illustrates how, after a life-altering tragedy, a person's needs for shelter and food can be met, but when the needs to give and receive love, and feel a sense of belonging are unmet, the greater needs for achieving self-esteem and knowing the personal power of emotional freedom is stunted.

Brandon's Story

Until the age of 6, Brandon lived a blessed life. A couple of weeks after his 7th birthday, Brandon's father, a truck driver, announced that he'd gotten a new job and the family was moving from New Orleans to Texas. Brandon remembers his mom having to pry him and his two older siblings out of their grandmother's arms and the three of them crying inconsolably throughout the whole seven and a half hour car ride.

Two weeks after arriving in Texas, a drunk driver ran a red light, killing his mother on her way home from the grocery store.

Their father, once happy and outgoing—now sullen and withdrawn, brought the three children back to New Orleans to be raised by their maternal grandparents. When he wasn't working, he used alcohol to excess. When he drank he would get easily angered, especially when Brandon and his brother got loud or horsed around. That's when the belt would come out. His older brother usually got the brunt of their father's anger but really neither of them was spared the beatings.

No one in his family ever talked about Brandon's mom or what happened to her. It was as though she had never existed. The pain and unresolved mourning, the lack of emotional support and not having any one with whom to acknowledge the void his mother's death created, left Brandon feeling isolated. He became angry, and it kept him from being able to meet his greater needs to have healthy self-esteem and appreciation.

Brandon's story asks that you assess your own wants and needs and the attention you were given, or that you gave to them, at various points in your life. Once Brandon understood the impact of his father's trauma on his own life, the feeling of empathy allowed for a reconnection, and resulted in healing.

"OF NEEDS"

Marshall Rosenberg, the founder of the Center for Nonviolent Communication, developed a method to address the awareness illuminated through his work: That all interpersonal conflict in our world arises because of unmet needs and feelings.

The method is known as nonviolent communication, a form of communication that allows you to address needs and feelings in a nonviolent way.

The practice of nonviolent communication requires that before you engage, you learn to reflect on how you are, without blaming or criticizing, and then receive your knowledge of self without blame or criticism. This requires that you observe (see, hear, remember or imagine) free from evaluation of what it is you are experiencing and empathize with what you are experiencing with your senses.

Once you have observed others in a non-judgmental way you then check in with how you are feeling (emotion or sensation rather than thought in relation to what you observed), again making room to empathize with how you are feeling in relation to what you've observed. Once the feelings are identified, you can work towards meeting the needs that arise as a result of your feelings.

The "OF NEEDS" is a tool for group discussion about needs, and, about managing emotions. Here is a link to the tool followed by a description of how it is used: http://www.echoparenting.org/wp-content/uploads/2012/04/week5_Ofneeds.pdf

O = Observe	What is happening? What are you seeing? What are you observing? Observe what is happening without judgment.
F = Feelings	What might the person be feeling? There may be many feelings.
N = Needs	What might the person be in need of? Remember, all feelings spring from needs.
E = Engage	Pay attention to your body, tone of voice. Are you entering the situation with curiosity?
E = Empathy	Put yourself in the other person's shoes.
D = Develop	Brainstorm…as you develop "the big picture."
S = Solutions	The solutions honor and respect the person's feelings and needs.

The "OF NEEDS" tool can be distributed to the class for review and discussion before the role-play exercise.

Role Play

To put OF NEEDS into practice, invite a volunteer to explain a problem (just the problem, not the solution) that he or she experienced in the past week, then facilitate a role play scene where two participants act out the issue. When the skit has been played to the point of waiting-for-a-solution, ask the two participants to freeze.

At that moment, ask these questions to the group and allow answers to be given:

1. What are the factors that led to this moment?
2. What in the lives of these two characters is affecting this moment?
3. What are you observing?
4. What are the unseen needs or wants under those feelings?
5. How can a healthy solution to this problem be created?

When a good solution is decided upon by group consensus, the two actors then act it out.

The Emotional Impact of Flowers

A team of researchers explored the link between flowers and life satisfaction in a 10-month study of participants' behavioral and emotional responses to receiving flowers (https://liliumflorals.com/blog/flowers-contribute-to-emotional-health/). The results showed that flowers are a natural and healthful moderator of moods.

In the research study, all participants expressed "true" or "excited" smiles upon receiving flowers, demonstrating extraordinary delight and gratitude. This reaction was universal, occurring in all age groups. Study participants reported feeling less depressed, anxious and agitated after receiving flowers, and demonstrated a higher sense of enjoyment and life satisfaction.

"Common sense tells us that flowers make us happy," said Jeanette Haviland-Jones, Ph.D., a professor of psychology at Rutgers University. "Now, science shows that not only do flowers make us happier than we know, they have strong positive effects on our emotional well-being."

The study also explored where in their homes people display flowers. The arrangements were placed in common areas of the home that were open to visitors. "Flowers bring about positive emotional feelings in those who enter a room," said Dr. Haviland-Jones. "They make the space more welcoming and create a sharing atmosphere."

After introducing this research to the class, give them each a flower. If possible, give the flowers as a surprise, then talk about how the class members feel about the flowers having had an immediate impact on their happiness.

Words and/or Images about Anger

Discuss flowers as symbols of healthy, positive emotional wellbeing and then finish with a writing exercise to analyze anger in relation to happiness.

Allow 15 to 20 minutes to write or draw a personal expression of anger. Ask what created that feeling of anger. Was it righteous or unjustified anger? Where were they when the incident occurred? How did their body feel in that moment? Was the incident resolved?

Then ask them to write or draw something about how they felt when receiving an unexpected gift, such as the flower each one received.

The Power of Observation and Awareness of What's Hidden

Anybody can become angry—that is easy, but to be angry with the right person and to the right degree and at the right time and for the right purpose, and in the right way—is not within everybody's power and is not easy.

~ ARISTOTLE ~

Aims and Intentions
- Learn to use powers of observation
- Rebecca's story

Tools and/or Exercises
- Observation tray exercise
- The natural state of awareness
- How to look within
- The Golden Rule and The Platinum Rule
- Words and/or images about observation

Materials
- Several (20-30) small, diverse items for observation tray (coin, pebble, key, etc., and tray)
- Pens or pencils and paper or journals

Observation is a useful skill that is possible to develop and improve at any time in life. It's more than just an ability to find a character or hidden figure in a cartoon; it is a life skill that requires patience to gain a way of seeing that is not clouded by stress, anger, or other limitations. It is also important to pay attention to what might be unseen. You can "see" what is unseen by using the skill of intuition.

As you read Rebecca's story, pay attention to what her anger prevents her from seeing in the background of her life.

Rebecca's Story

Rebecca grew up in a broken home and was raised by her aunt because her mother was an alcoholic and a drug addict. She never knew her father. Her aunt was a strict Christian, and Rebecca remembers being allowed to go out after church to a movie or to have pizza with her friends, but never to go to parties.

Although her aunt deeply loved her, Rebecca felt emptiness—until she met Chris. They were in the church choir together; at 14, Rebecca was four years younger than Chris. One thing they shared was the lack of a father's influence and love. Rebecca and Chris conceived a daughter who was born when Rebecca was 15. The aunt, in an attempt to protect Rebecca, threatened to have Chris arrested for statutory rape if he ever set foot in her house or tried to be part of Rebecca's life.

By the time she was 27, Rebecca was on her own with three children, and, Child Protective Services was threatening to take her kids away. That is when she was assigned to the parenting program I taught.

When Rebecca was nearing completion of the program, she handed me a letter from her 13-year-old daughter: "I want to thank you for your tips and helping my mom be strong and more sensible," she wrote. "I see my mom more sure of making good choices and of course of being more patient with us, she works a lot and comes home tired but she makes us food. I love her when she leaves the pain in her and also the stress she had in her heart from my dad."

One of the greatest benefits of observation is the ability to witness what someone else is experiencing, working towards, overcoming, or improving. Rebecca's life may have been chaotic, but she was raising a daughter who—at a very young age—had profound powers of observation, and they served as a compliment to her mother's healing.

Observation Skills

This "observation" is a challenge, but it's also fun. Gather between 20 and 30 objects, diverse but similar in size (such as a penny, a paper clip, a key, a rock, etc.) and put them on a tray. Hand out paper and pencils, and then put the tray out where people can observe it for about two minutes. Then put the tray away (or cover the items with a cloth), and give two minutes to write a list of items observed and remembered.

This exercise is much more difficult than it seems but it demonstrates the power of observation and memory. This is not a competition, but it does allow people to compare what they saw with what was observed by others. It is a beautiful exercise in perception and "seeing how others see."

The Natural State of Awareness

Lock Kelly, founder of the Open-Hearted Awareness Institute said, "The natural state of awareness is already in us," but is not culturally supported. From the time you are born, you are taught to see yourself as separate from objects. You are trained to focus on the mind/intellect, and to see with your ego.

As the ego develops, it discovers the flight, fright, or freeze states. Imagine a young child standing near a hot stove. A parent or caretaker alerts the child and teaches about the danger of fire and heat. Three things can happen next: The child trusts the warning and moves away from the danger (fright), gets stalled in fear (freeze), or tests (fights) it.

How to Look Within

In this link is a 5:19-minute video about a simple practice that teaches you how to look within and observe yourself: www.youtube.com/watch?v=VvEuWoRyD9Q. It came from author Loch Kelly's book, *Shift into Freedom: The Science & Practice of Open-Hearted Awareness*.

The Golden Rule and the Platinum Rule

The power of observation makes a great deal of difference when one person is relating to another person. Tony Alessandra, Ph.D. took the Golden Rule ('treat others the way you yourself wish to be treated') a little further with his idea of "The Platinum Rule." This is all about treating others the way you observe how they want to be treated. For more information: www.alessandra.com/abouttony/aboutpr.asp. Alessandra's website says, "The goal of The Platinum Rule is personal chemistry and productive relationships. You do not have to change your personality. You do not have to roll over and submit to others. You simply have to understand what drives people and recognize your options for dealing with them."

Individuals such as Tony Alessandra and Marshall Rosenberg recognize and understand the importance of learning to observe situations and people to identify their feelings and possible underlying needs. These insights enable you to develop or discover healthy solutions towards helping to meet those needs.

Words and/or Images about Observation

Think back to the observation tray exercise to remember how well you did. Then draw or write about how you plan to use or improve your powers of internal awareness and observation.

Attachment Styles

*Our bodies and our brains are storing memories of
early experiences, creating patterns that deeply affect
our relationships and our behaviors in adult life.*

~ DIANE POOLE HELLER, PH.D. ~

Aims and Intentions
* Sergio's story
* Attachment theory—understanding the essential bond

Tools and/or Exercises
* A window of opportunity
* Four attachment styles
* Healthy attachment exercise
* The "Still Face" experiment
* Words and/or images about attachment styles
* Compassionate witness exercise
* "Head Hold" exercise

Materials
* "Still Face" experiment videos: www.youtube.com/watch?v=6czxW4R9w2g and www.youtube.com/watch?v=apzXGEbZht0
* "What is Your Attachment Style?" from PsychAlive: www.psychalive.org/what-is-your-attachment-style/
* Capacitar information on the "Head Hold:" https://capacitar.org/
* Pens or pencils and paper or journals
* Post-it® large tablet and Sharpie® marker

How well a child bonds with parents or caregivers influences his or her entire lifetime. An understanding of early attachment experiences and styles and how they influence adult behaviors is necessary to learn. Watch for this truth in Sergio's story.

Sergio's Story

Sergio sports a large tattoo of the Virgin Mary on his right forearm. Like many who grow up in chaotic and violent homes, Sergio has very few memories of the time before age 7. His first memory is one of being beaten by both parents. They bloodied his face; a scar on his lip is from that incident, but Sergio cannot remember why he was tortured.

When Sergio was 8, his maternal grandmother was given custody. She did the best she could to provide for and nurture him and he remembers his grandfather teaching him the value of work. Occasionally his father would visit, always with a different woman.

Sergio was 15 when his father offered to take him to a whorehouse and told him that if he wanted to have sex with a woman, he should just take her. Sergio remembers not knowing what to say or do.

Love, partnership, and parenthood happened for Sergio at the ages of 20, 23, and 32. His lover, who was five years older than he, birthed his three children.

The day Sergio joined the parenting group, his oldest child turned 15.

Sergio realized that he needed to come into relationship with his children and be more to them just a provider of shelter and food.

Attachment Theory— Understanding the Essential Bond

In order to understand the word "heal," and the lifelong process of "healing," you must observe how your childhood traumas still influence your adult experiences before you can make changes. Many people live out unresolved traumas, and it influences everything they do.

In order to grow you must be willing to engage in transformation. Transformation is the process of changing something in relation to its polar opposite. In the transformation from a traumatic state to a peaceful state, there are fundamental changes in your neurobiology. The nervous system swings between immobility and fluidity, emotions fluctuate between fear and courage, and perception shifts between narrow-mindedness and receptivity.

Your nervous system has the capacity to self-regulate. Emotions can be experiences that lift you up rather than bring you down. When you broaden your perceptions, you learn from your experiences. You can engage in healing yourself, but it requires more than the alleviation of symptoms. It requires transformation.

Window of Opportunity

In order to transform, you begin by changing your narrative. It's not always an easy endeavor but it can be done. Suspending, addressing, and changing the traumatic ways of being that your childhood relationships engrained in you requires attention, intention, focus and persistence. You'll take chances, but you'll build both fortitude and faith to examine, transform, and expand your sense of self. A by-product of this work is that you'll gain insight into overall human behavior.

Four Attachment Styles

Your amazing brain has a quality scientists call "neuroplasticity." It is the brain's ability to change. Humans are not biological automatons controlled by genes. All your patterns and programs are not manifested at the moment of conception. You are dynamic, fluid, always changing, and your organs are capable of adapting to almost any type of environment. Even the programming in your genes can change and be modified by your experiences and the environment's effects on your body.

Dan Siegel, M.D., Ph.D., defined four attachment styles: secure, avoidant, ambivalent/anxious, and disorganized. Here is a link for more information on Dr. Siegel's work: www.drdansiegel.com, and here is a link to "What is Your Attachment Style?" from PsychAlive: www.psychalive.org/what-is-your-attachment-style/.

Secure From the time infants are six months to two years of age, they form an emotional attachment to a caregiver who is attuned to their needs. In the ideal situation, a caregiver is sensitive, consistent, and responsive in all interactions with the infant and child.

During the second year, children see the adult as a secure base from which to explore the world and become more independent. A child in this type of relationship is securely attached.

Avoidant Emotionally unavailable adults are insensitive to and unaware of the needs of their children. They give little in the way of positive, negative, or neutral responses to a child when it is hurting or distressed. These parents discourage crying and encourage independence. Children of these types of caregivers develop into "little adults" who close in, and take care of themselves. They pull away from needing anything from anyone, and act as if they are self-contained. They have formed an avoidant attachment with a nonresponsive adult who oversees their care.

Ambivalent/Anxious Some adults are inconsistently attuned to children. At times, their responses are appropriate and nurturing, but at other times, they are intrusive and insensitive. Children exposed to this kind of caregiving or parenting are confused and insecure, not knowing what type of treatment to expect. They often feel suspicious and distrustful of the caregiver, but at the same time, they act clingy and desperate. These children have an ambivalent/anxious attachment with an unpredictable parent or caregiver.

Disorganized This occurs when a parent or caregiver is abusive to a child, and the child experiences physical trauma, emotional cruelty, and frightening behavior as being life-threatening. This child is caught in a terrible dilemma—the child's survival instincts tell him or her to flee to safety, but safety is supposed to be with the very person who is terrifying the child. The attachment figure is the source of the child's distress. In these situations, children typically disassociate. They detach from what is happening to them, and what they are experiencing is blocked from their consciousness. Children in this conflicted state have disorganized attachments with fearsome authority figures, the people who are also supposed to nurture them.

Healthy Attachment

Using information on the four attachment styles, create a Post-it® sheet as a visual guide to use for a group discussion:

Child Attachment	Adult Narrative
Secure	Secure
Fearful	Avoidance and Distrust
Ambivalent or Anxious	Preoccupied
Dismissive	Grief and Unresolved Trauma

"Still Face Experiment"

Watch a 2:48-minute video about the "Still Face Experiment" with Edward Tronick, Ph.D. at www.youtube.com/watch?v=apzXGEbZht0. If there is time, you may also view this one, filmed in 2016, and with dads: www.youtube.com/watch?v=6czxW4R9w2g; it is 4:28-minutes long. Ask the group to create pairs for five minutes of discussion about what the videos made them feel, think, and need. After this sharing, return to a large group and allow anyone to share significant insights.

Words and/or Images about Attachment Styles

In words or pictures, with pencils and paper, explore your childhood attachment style with curiosity, openness, acceptance, and love. Work towards recognizing and gaining insight into the attachment styles of your caregivers. Ask yourself how your early experiences shaped, are shaping, and will continue to shape your life.

Be a Compassionate Witness

In any interaction with another human being, there is the possibility of connection or of turning away. According to the philosophy behind the African tradition of Ubuntu, there exists a common bond between all people and it is through this bond, and interaction with fellow human beings, that a person discovers their own human qualities. It is the essence of being human: "I am human because I belong. I am what I am because of who I'm with."

The Golden Rule, or law of reciprocity, says to treat others as you wish to be treated. It is a concept that occurs in some form in all religions and ethical traditions. It demands that each individual see, empathize with, and be a witness to the other.

For this exercise, the group splits into pairs. After partnerships form, lead them through three deep breaths for relaxation. Next, ask them to take a body inventory. Tell them to ground themselves in their chairs, making sure to firmly plant their feet on the ground. If they feel tension in a specific area, have them breathe into that area and slowly relax. The goal is for everyone to be present to themselves before engaging as a pair.

Make sure the chairs are about three and a half feet apart and that the participants sit facing each other. They do not talk or touch. Have them focus their eyes between their partner's brows so that they can see both pupils simultaneously. Tell them it is fine to blink, but to not close their eyes, or to look away.

The only task for the next five minutes is to be present with the partner and look into one another's eyes. To really see and feel connected to someone, you need to be still in mind and body. Pay attention to your breath. It should be slow until it is almost unnoticeable. You will undergo all manner of discomfort during your encounter, including sore muscles, dry eyes and niggling thoughts. Don't dwell on them.

Ask them to connect with what is alive in themselves and ask that they open their heart to how they feel. Imagine what the person across from them is feeling or thinking. Go back to self: What are you feeling or thinking? What could your partner need in this moment? What do you need?

Let yourself be seen. Let yourself be vulnerable. Open your heart even though there is no surety. Be present and allow for gratitude and joy to enter, appreciate that you are enough, that you are perfect as you are, and that your partner is all that, too.

This kind of purposeful eye contact elicits avoidance behavior in many species, but humans are exquisitely attuned to it. Even newborns will look longer at people who are staring straight at them than they will at those with averted eyes.

This exercise teaches that you need to look at your loved ones more than you probably do, but in this moment, gazing into the eyes of strangers is more transformative. It is one of the most powerful experiences you can have. Deep awareness of the other person is healing.

Once the five minutes are up allow some time to unpack feelings and express the experiences with one another.

Capacitar's "Head Hold"

This practice consists of several simple energy holds that may be done on the self or on another person for anxiety, emotional or physical pain, traumatic memories, strong emotions, such as anger or fear, insomnia, and for deep relaxation. Through the energy of your hands, you have the power to bring profound peace, harmony and healing to body, mind and emotions.

Still in pairs, now one person is seated, the other is standing. The one standing asks permission to touch, then places a hand lightly on the partner's head, high on the forehead, with one hand. With the other hand, lightly hold the base of the skull at the back of the neck. If someone fears touch because of pain, or a history of abuse, the head holds may be done off the body, without touch, in the energy fields. Always ask permission when you do any practice that involves touching another person's skin.

The energy of one partner's hands connects with parts of the seated partner's brain related to memories and emotions. The holds can be done for several minutes each, accompanied by deep abdominal breathing to promote greater release. The touch is to remain very light. Remind the person sitting to relax and breathe deeply. After five minutes, have the partners switch.

You Are Not Your Traumas

The past is gone, the future is not yet here, and if we do not go back to ourselves in the present moment, we cannot be in touch with life.

~ THICH NHAT HANH ~

Aims and Intentions
- Sankofa bird story
- Patricia's story

Tools and/or Exercises
- Sankofa bird drawing exercise
- Ropes, stones, flowers exercise

Materials
- Guided meditation text to use in class and take home
- Ropes, stones, flowers
- Pens or pencils and paper or journals

The story of the Sankofa bird comes from West Africa. This bird is used to teach a lesson about remembering painful experiences. In the story that has passed down for ages, the Sankofa is a mythic bird that flies forward while looking backward while holding an egg (symbolizing the future) in its mouth.

The bird's peculiar way of flying teaches that it is necessary to look back at one's the roots in order to move forward. In order to achieve full potential, people need to be wise enough to reach back and gather the best of what the past has to teach. Whatever you've lost, forgotten, not chosen, or been stripped of, can be reclaimed, revived, preserved, and perpetuated.

The story Patricia tells involves her traumatic past, anxious present, and future healing.

Patricia's Story

Patricia had a chaotic childhood full of violence and struggle. She told the group she thought everyone automatically knew to lay down on the floor when gunshots rang out because, having learned to do so at an early age, it was natural to her. The environment Patricia experienced taught her that in order to live, she must fight to survive by any means necessary.

Her parents had a history of drug addiction. Her best friend and hero was her brother Freddy, two years her senior. Patricia was constantly praying that Freddy would not get shot, killed, or locked up because, like her other two older siblings, Freddy was in a gang.

Another important person who brought a little light into Patricia's world was her middle school teacher and basketball coach, Ms. D. The compassion and caring relationship that they developed for each other gave Patricia a reason to stay in school. Both on the basketball court and in the classroom, Patricia tried her best to meet Ms. D's expectations and to not disappoint her.

One day at school Patricia got into a fight with another girl over a boy they both liked. As the school police broke it up, Patricia saw Ms. D standing outside her classroom crying. It was the last time Patricia ever fought in school.

The day Patricia turned 14, Freddy and one of his gang friends were arrested for a gang shooting. Even though he was only 16, he was charged as an adult and received a 20-year prison sentence. The day he was taken away, Patricia said her life spun out of control. Freddy's life was one loss too many, and Patricia gave up on herself and decided to sell drugs. She lost any motivation she had for school and skipped classes until 10th grade, when she dropped out.

At the time of printing this book, Patricia is finishing her undergraduate education and plans to get a master's degree in counseling and social work.

Sankofa Bird

Ask students to draw an image of the Sankofa bird. As they draw, ask them to think about what it means to remember their own past history for a better understanding of life in the present. Beneath the drawing of the Sankofa bird, ask students to write about where they grew up—to describe housing and landscape memories. Then ask them to draw themselves as a child surrounded by images of those who influenced them. Ask them to pay attention to the feelings attached to those memories and let them be reflected in the drawings.

Ropes. Stones. Flowers.

Each person is given a length of rope (at least 24"). The rope symbolizes the timeline of his or her life with one end of the rope marking their birth. Lay the ropes out on a smooth surface, leaving one end of the rope in the shape of a spiral to represent the future. Now give them flowers and stones of different sizes and colors.

The flowers represent joyful, happy times in their lives; stones represent sad, fearful, and painful times. Each person is asked to place flowers and stones along the rope "timeline" to represent significant events they experienced.

Save the materials used for this exercise for the next segment.

Narrating the Future for Your Generations

The practice of forgiveness is our most important contribution to the healing of the world.

~ MARIANNE WILLIAMSON ~

Aims and Intentions
- Pair memories of the past with imagining the future
- Breath and body awareness
- Fernando's story

Tools and/or Exercises
- Breath, body, brain exercise
- The six "A" words – attachment, acceptance, attention, affection, appreciation, autonomy
- Guided meditation
- Words and/or images exercise about good memories

Materials
- Pens or pencils and paper or journals
- Ropes, stones, and flowers
- Glue or threaded needles or stickers
- Post-it® large tablet and Sharpie® marker

When you hold on to memories of pain you hand down a suitcase packed with trauma from generation to generation. To recognize your suitcase and unpack it requires courage and strong self-esteem. A person who was not exposed to safety and fairness in childhood must summon the desire and energy to figure out how to build both as an adult.

Sexual abuse was an unspoken trauma in Fernando's life and it led to his presence in the group. He had children who were going to be part of this legacy, until....

Fernando's Story

Sitting across from the members of the group, I found myself listening to Fernando share his story with a partner. During class time together it was clear to me that Fernando looked up to and trusted the man with whom I had paired him. Fernando's face lit up as he conveyed the happiness he felt after the call from his social worker at child protective services letting him know that he and his wife had fulfilled all constraints and conditions and were on the road to regaining custody of their 3-year-old son.

Fernando recalled how hard the last two years had been with his son in foster care, an experience made more painful by the fact that as a child, he too had been removed from his parents' custody. "Both my parents were physically abusive. My father sexually abused me."

The man sitting across from him was at a loss as to how to respond. Fortunately, the pair share rule requires that one talk and the other just listens.

Fernando shared his concerns over being able to hold onto his son. He didn't know what to do about his wife and her anger issues. She also struggled with a drinking problem. In fact, just last week he had to break up a physical altercation she got into with one of her cousins after they'd had a few too many beers.

Listening to this 23-year-old young man, I thought about his infant son. My hope for his future lay in the belief that through this work Fernando would gain better coping skills and improved functioning tools and, in so doing, prevent his child from experiencing his accumulation of ACEs—and more.

Because he was given information about the science behind ACEs, Fernando had an opportunity to break the chains of secrecy and taboo that bound his child's experience to his own.

Breath and Body Awareness

In his book, *Man's Search for Meaning,* Viktor Frankl, a concentration camp survivor and psychotherapist, discovered that one of the most important factors in restoring psychological wellbeing for those who have experienced trauma is finding a sense of meaning and purpose. This takes asking difficult questions such as "What happened to me?" and "Why do I feel this way?"

If a child is not taught to self-soothe and regulate their emotions, they must learn to do so as an adult if they are to experience the reason for both positive and negatives experiences. Knowing that healing is a continual process requires maintenance of an attitude that enables it to be done—and it requires work.

Trauma therapist Peter A. Levine, Ph.D. observed that when trauma strikes it is like a meteorite that fell from space and left a huge impact on the Earth. In this metaphor, you are gently rafting down the river of life and a huge meteoric trauma impacts just outside the containing boundaries of your river. This creates a deep hole that the water from the river rushes into, like water going down a drain. It creates a spinning vortex that makes the water move faster and faster and becomes inescapable as you spiral down the hole. This vortex draws you in and sucks you down if you get near to it.

This is very much what it is like for people who have unresolved trauma. Anytime they get into a situation that closely resembles the trauma event they experienced, they feel that they are in extreme danger and unconsciously enter into the fight-or-flight response. The objective is to get away from the source of threat. All of your muscles prepare for this escape by increasing their tension level; your heart rate and respiration increase, and your whole metabolic system is flooded with adrenaline. Blood is diverted to the muscles, away from the viscera. The goal is to run away; or if you feel you cannot escape, or if you perceive the individual trying to attack you is less strong than you, then you attack them. If you're cornered and it looks like you're going to be killed, you go into a state of shock, that is, catatonic immobility.

Breath, Body, Brain

Your respiratory system, usually involuntary, can also be voluntarily controlled. It regulates all the body's autonomic systems, including brain and heart function. Controlling and changing the way you breathe goes a long way towards getting you unstuck from the debilitating effects of central nervous system over-activation.

Sit in a comfortable position with the spine straight and head bowed slightly forward. Close your eyes and take a few deep breaths. Engage a slow, deep inhale; hold; a slow exhale. As you become aware of your breath, focus on the sensations in your body; restore your connection to your sensations.

Shift your attention to your body and the places where it is relaxed, the places holding tension. Start with your toes and as you move upward to each body part, ask, "Are you relaxed or are you tense?" Whenever you discover a tense area, exaggerate the tension slightly by saying, "I am tensing my neck muscles." Then release the added tightness as you say, "I now let go. I am safe. I no longer need to hold this tension."

All muscular tension is self-produced. Let the cause for the tension you hold reveal itself to you. What else can you do—beyond bringing attention to it—to change it? Each time you go through this breathing process, notice how relaxed you can get. Ask yourself: "What parts of my body come into awareness first? What parts am I less aware of?" Become aware of which components of your body you can feel easily and which ones have little sensation. Do you notice any difference between the right and left side of your body? Scan your body for any residual tension or discomfort and let it go with each exhalation.

Continue breathing and letting go for up to 10 minutes, allowing your breathing to take over as your mind and thoughts relax and drift.

The more you practice this breath exercise, the more useful it becomes. Let it be part of your daily routine and use it again whenever your tension rises. It will inform your reaction to whatever is causing an upset. Use it whenever you are aware of internal tension or stress. Use it to help you fall asleep. Everyone can benefit from it.

Once your nervous system is regulated through breath and body, you are better able to focus on the real work at hand. Your mind is hardwired to protect itself at all times. If your ego feels threatened or damaged, learn to avoid expending energy on fruitless actions. Instead, pause and reflect. This allows the space in your mind to choose the action that is best for yourself and others.

Catching yourself before you engage in an automatic or unconscious reaction is one of the greatest challenges of your life. Learn to pause and practice it consistently; it will change your default reaction. When self-discipline, moments of reflection, and mindfulness allow a moment of clarity, you choose how to best respond.

The Six "A" Words

Self-awareness requires that you open your heart, your feelings, to your needs, but also to the needs of others. These six "A" words serve as a useful tool. Use the Post-it tablet and marker to list them for discussion:

1. **Attachment** - the opposite of attachment is lack of connection
2. **Acceptance** - the opposite of acceptance is trying to change the person
3. **Attention** - the opposite of attention is refusal to listen, being emotionally and physically unavailable
4. **Affection** - the opposite of affection is being withdrawn, withholding love and touch
5. **Appreciation** - the opposite of appreciation is criticizing, humiliating
6. **Autonomy** - the opposite of autonomy is being controlling, demanding, manipulative

Using the Six "A" Words

Take some time to reflect on or discuss each word and its opposite. Ask yourself the following six questions:

1. How may these words help me to make wiser decisions?

2. How do they help me become more aware of what I am thinking and feeling?

3. How can these words help me to not place blame on external factors? How do these words empower me to be more loving and compassionate?

4. How do these words support me in being more empathetic and open?

5. How do these words and meanings enable me to learn from my mistakes?

6. Which of these words make me most comfortable or uncomfortable?

Emotional literacy involves increasing your vocabulary to describe emotions and then having the ability to connect with others using that vocabulary. There is a language of nonviolence; these words open the door to peace. Build an intention to integrate them into your life and practice paying attention to their meanings and opposite meanings.

Do this by visualizing the world environment you want to live in. Go through the six "A" words and look for examples of times you experienced these six needs having been met or not met.

Guided Meditation

Sit in a chair and get comfortable to prepare for a five-minute guided meditation. Begin by focusing on your breath, and as you breathe in repeat these words to yourself: "When I breathe in I can feel my body and mind becoming calm."

Exhale and in your mind say: "When I breathe out I smile."

As you sit and breathe in calm, breathe out happiness; be present to yourself and these sensations for a few moments.

Now say, "This is a wonderful moment. It is a joy to just be, to be safe, stable, and at ease."

Ask yourself if you feel peace and joy right now. If you do not feel peace and joy, ask when you think you will have peace and joy. What is preventing you from being happy right now?

If you are happy, ask, "Why am I happy right now? What might I do to continue this feeling of happiness beyond this moment?"

Sit with those thoughts; breathe slowly and steadily. Sit for five minutes in silence.

Words and/or Images about Good Memories

Use your memory to recall one of your "flower moments" from the rope-stones-flowers exercise. Write or draw the details of that moment to show how much it means to you. How was the moment you just recalled informed by the breath, body, and awareness work you just did in the meditation? Write or draw your answer.

Recognizing Loss and the Process of Grief

*Our sorrows and wounds are healed only
when we touch them with compassion.*

~ BUDDHA ~

Aims and Intentions
* Understand grief as a gateway to a fuller and more loving understanding of all things in life, an opening to the realm of spirit and soul energies
* Learn about resources for recognizing, processing and managing grief
* Denise's story

Tools and/or Exercises
* The definitions of grief and depression
* Five stages of grief
* Grief mask exercise
* Resources for dealing with grief (www.grief.com)

Materials
* Mask materials: balloons, newspaper, plain paper, glue, water, paint and paintbrushes, straight pins, scissors
* Link to craft of mask making: https://www.youtube.com/watch?v=FCiYNE_hmNg
* Post-it® large tablet and Sharpie® marker

The work this book demands of readers and group participants is meant to be transformative and can lead to a profound personal metamorphosis. As individuals transform from worm to the chrysalis stage and into butterflies, they attain skills and tools to make more effective and healthier choices. They experience viewing the world with more freedom and love, and without suffering from the vigilance fear demands. They no longer believe that only the worst can happen.

However, they also experience a loss—the loss of their former fearful self.

This loss leads to a feeling of uncertainty about where they stand. Acknowledge and allow them to process this kind of loss by helping them to understand the grief process.

Denise wanted to regain custody of her daughter while being unemployed and battling depression. Her sense of humor was a shield that could not protect her from her grief and sense of loss.

Denise's Story

On Valentine's Day, she came into our meeting room with a string of beautiful helium balloons and handed one to each of us. As I received mine I reflected on how those with the least to give are frequently the ones that give the most. There was also the moment of awareness that the act of giving lifted Denise's spirit, a moment of light and respite.

Denise was the group's clown, always one to offer a joke. Beyond that mask of humor, the pain and darkness she carried was still apparent. Her struggles with drug and alcohol addiction, the loss of her daughter to the foster care system, the inconsistent low paying and menial work, her estrangement from family, the 52-week domestic violence classes for which she had to pay... all these daily pressures led to a heavy cross to bear and manifested in depression and grief.

Denise was referred to a therapist after the classes ended so that she could continue the work of healing, and be a better mother to her child. She needed tools that were unique to her situation.

Definition of Depression

The *Merriam-Webster Dictionary* (www.merriam-webster.com) defines grief: "grief: noun \'grēf\ 1 obsolete : grievance 2 a: deep and poignant distress caused by or as if by bereavement *his grief over his son's death* b: a cause of such suffering *life's joys and griefs* 3 a: an unfortunate outcome : disaster —used chiefly in the phrase *come to grief* b: mishap, misadventure c: trouble, annoyance *enough grief for one day* d: annoying or playful criticism *getting grief from his friends.*"

In her book, *Glossary of QuantumPathic Terms,* energy healer Sherry Anshara defines depression as, "An emotion that is the deepest disappointment in one's own self."

Depression and grief are large and difficult emotions. These emotions have many layers—from profound sadness due to the loss of a feeling, death of a person or destruction of a thing, to a wistful feeling of missing something wished for but never received. When these feelings are looked at through a positive lens, they can be used as a gateway for opening the heart and mind to new information that can lead to growth and transcendence.

The Five Stages of Grief

The stages of grief as defined by Elizabeth Kubler Ross, M.D. and David Kessler in their book *On Grief & Grieving: Finding the Meaning of Grief through the Five Stages of Loss* are listed here to be written on a Post-it® sheet for group discussion.

> **Denial**
> **Anger**
> **Bargaining**
> **Depression**
> **Acceptance**

See www.grief.com for guidance and free resources on dealing with grief.

Grief Mask

Think of a mask. It hides the reality of true emotions. When people experience loss, they often put up a brave front. They pretend to be strong when they are emotionally weak and vulnerable on the inside.

Recall a time of grief. How did you process it? Did you put up a front, or put on a mask to cover the raw emotion of grief?

Making a grief mask is like creating a sculpture. Creating something of beauty from sadness often helps a person access truth and express it in a new way. When you agree to make a grief mask, you step into your powers of creativity. https://www.youtube.com/watch?v=FCiYNE_hmNg

Set out the materials (balloons, newspaper, plain paper, flour, water, straight pins, paints and paintbrushes). Inflate a balloon. The size of the inflated balloon is the size of your mask. A smaller balloon will be easier to work with. It's fine if you just have newspaper, but it's even better if you can provide plain paper, like printer paper. Grab a whole bunch of sheets and some flour and water for your paste. Here are step-by-step instructions:

1. Lay down some newspaper to catch drips and make clean up easier.
2. Rip the rest of the newspapers and the solid paper into strips or squares, depending on the size of your balloon. You'll need enough for at least three layers and whatever molding you may want to do.

3. Create a paste with 2 cups (220 g) flour and 1 cup (200 ml) water. If you do not have flour, you can use two parts white glue and one part water. Mix it well. The paste will be easiest to use if it is in a shallow tray or wide rimmed bowl.

4. Dip a piece of paper into the paste and let it soak a bit, making sure the paper is completely covered with the paste. Remove the excess paste by scraping it along the side of the tray or bowl.

5. The first layer of newspaper should be placed vertically on the balloon, the second horizontally, and so forth. Apply the blank paper in between newspaper layers to make it easy to see where you've already gone.

6. If you'd like to mold on features, do so now. The beauty of *papier mâché* is that the strips can mold into virtually any shape. You can form eyebrows, cheekbones, or lips rather easily.

7. Set your balloon on its side to dry. Make sure that the newspaper is securely attached to the balloon or else your mask may come apart. This drying stage may take several hours.

8. Pop the balloon with a needle or pin. For safety reasons, be sure to pop it away from your face. You now have the base of your mask!

9. Use scissors to cut the newspaper ball in half. Depending on how much of the balloon you covered, you may end up with two separate masks, one large mask, or a mask that you want to shave down in size.

10. Start cutting holes. You will want two for eyes, at least one for the nose, and possibly one for the mouth.

11. Decorate your mask.

Resources for Dealing with Grief

During a time of grief, asking for help is often difficult. Knowing that many resources that provide comfort are available is a tool you can use to bring balance back to your nervous and emotional systems while suffering a loss. There are two kinds of resources: external and internal.

Using two blank Post-it® sheets write "External Resources" on one and "Internal Resources" on the other. Talk about the two kinds:

- External resources include positive experiences, people, places, spiritual guides, activities, skills, hobbies, and animals
- Internal resources include positive experiences, values and beliefs that validate and give meaning to life; also personal qualities like kindness, compassion and humor

Ask for examples from the group and write them on the Post-It® sheets. During the discussion have the class talk about the feelings they have about these resources and how they have used them.

Kintsukuroi: To Repair by Using Gold

When we love, we always strive to become better than we are. When we strive to become better than we are, everything around us becomes better too.

~ PAULO COELHO ~

Aims and Intentions
- See healing as a process of repair
- Jacob's story

Tools and/or Exercises
- Kintsukuroi exercise (www.philipchircop.wordpress.com/2013/11/10/the-fable-of-kintsukuroi/)
- How to re-set the nervous system

Materials
- Ceramic bowls or cups
- Hammers or small, blunt objects (rocks, handle of a butter knife, etc.)
- Paper or plastic bags
- Glue
- Gold glitter
- Sharpie® markers

The Japanese have a word for a special kind of repair: kintsukuroi. When they mend broken objects, they aggrandize the damage by filling the cracks with gold.

They believe that when something has suffered damage and has a history it becomes more beautiful. You can read the fable that led to this practice by clicking on this link: https://philipchircop.wordpress.com/2013/11/10/the-fable-of-kint-sukuroi/.

Getting high was Jacob's self-soothing practice. Being in the group helped him realize that escape is not a route towards healing.

Jacob's Story

A part time drug dealer trafficking in the sale of marijuana, Jacob had been smoking pot since his early teens and had developed a dependency on it. One evening, a couple came over to purchase some drugs and heard screams coming from his kitchen. Walking onto the porch through the opened screen door, they witnessed Jacob throwing his wife onto the floor. They called the police.

As our group mended the broken bowls and lined them with gold, Jacob opened up and shared stories from his childhood. When he turned 12 his father, who was also a drug dealer, was arrested and sentenced to 15 years in prison. Jacob was fatherless in his teen and young adult years. While his father was away, many men paraded through his house. Some were nice but he knew that most of them were using his mother, and he was angry with her.

After telling us that he didn't respect women much (he thought they only wanted him for money), Jacob said, "I know my baby's mama is just in it for what I give her. She never once visited me when I was locked up."

Holding the pieces of the broken bowl in his hand he got emotional as he shared that his son had just turned 12 and he didn't want to repeat the sins of his father and abandon his son. Jacob didn't want to end up locked up and have his boy grow up without a father. To pull himself together, Jacob grabbed the glue and worked to reconstruct his cracked bowl. "Gonna have to take it a day at a time. Gonna be there for him. I know that," he said.

When Jacob stopped getting high, he worked to end the vicious cycle. He started spending quality time with his son and being a different father than his own father had been.

Kintsukuroi

Place the cup or bowl in a paper or plastic bag, then tap the bag gently but with enough force to break the cup into several pieces. Remove broken pieces from bag. On the interior of each piece write the words that express your trauma. Reconstruct the cup using gold glitter glue. Once the cup is put back together, write descriptive words on the outside of the cup that identify your resilience.

Once this activity is complete, break into pairs to discuss the cup repair activity. Remember, the brain has plasticity; it can heal itself. Reflect on how coming through the experience of brokenness and repair, people earn strength and become more beautiful. Share with one another how it feels to know that trauma is like the gold glitter used to repair the broken cup or bowl; it informs one's capacity for empathy, compassion and resilience.

How to Reset the Body's Nervous System

When your emotions feel broken or out-of-control, when your body is suffering the effects of stress, you can use one of these methods of repair:

1. Drink a glass of water.

2. Look around the room or your outdoor environment. Pay attention to anything that catches your eye. Describe it in as much detail as you can remember or tell yourself a story about it.

3. Name six colors you see nearby. Then name those things that were the colors you chose.

4. Count backwards from 20 as you walk at a slow speed. Notice objects in your path and touch their surfaces to get a sense of different textures on your skin.

5. Close your eyes; feel and guess the temperature of the air that surrounds you.

6. Close your eyes and pay attention to the sounds you hear.

7. Take a walk and pay attention to the movement of your arms and legs; how your feet are making contact with the ground.

8. Put your hands against a wall and lean in with all your weight then notice your muscles.

9. Stand up, cross your right ankle over your left; put your arms in front and cross your left arm over your right arm; clasp your hands and draw them into your chest; hold the pose for a minute while taking a few deep breaths; then come out of the pose in a slow, thoughtful way.

Choose and practice a few of these tools on your own. When complete, find a partner and share your experiences.

Change Is a Process, Not a One-Time Event

There is nothing permanent except change.

~ HERACLITUS ~

Aims and Intentions
* Understand that to heal is to transform
* Vicki's story

Tools and/or Exercises
* The transtheoretical model
* The five stages of change
* Words and/or images about change
* Tai Chi energy

Materials
* Link: "The Transtheoretical Model of Change" by Proschaska, DiClemente and Norcross, https://www.prochange.com/transtheoretical-model-of-behavior-change
* A system to play music that inspires change (phone, tape recorder)
* Pens or pencils and paper or journals
* Link to background music playlists: https://danspira.com/2014/05/12/14-songs-about-change-a-trainers-personal-playlist/
* Post-it® large tablet and a Sharpie® marker

Everyone is constantly changing. Everyone is constantly fighting change. The recognition of this fact of life relates to how people make change for the better, while still being part of the process of change.

Running was a part of Vicki's lifestyle. Although she needed emotional support, she ran…and ran…and ran…until she stopped long enough to pay attention to ACEs science.

Vicki's Story

From the stories that Vicki shared about her mother, it was clear that her mom struggled with a mental health disorder. But in the culture and small town where Vicki grew up there were no services or even a common way to talk about mental health issues.

The oldest of three sisters, Vicki remembers being a little girl of 5 or 6, cowering on top of a bed as her enraged mom, holding a large fork used for grilling, tried to stab her little sister who had crawled under the bed. On the days when her mother wasn't angry or enraged, she was sad and crying. Usually on those days she would stay sequestered in her room, not even coming out to eat. During those times, Vicki assumed the role of caretaker, making sure she and her sisters were clothed, fed, and made it to school.

A bright light in Vicki's life was her mother's sister, Aunt Doris. Although Aunt Doris had a family of her own, she would often come by and care for Vicki and her sisters. Aunt Doris told Vicki that she was special and would do great things someday. Vicki could tell her aunt anything, share any problem or concern, and Doris would solve it.

Vicki got pregnant at 17, and her boyfriend wanted her to get an abortion. Aunt Doris convinced her to keep the baby, offering to do whatever was in her power to help with the care of the child. Vicki named the baby Doris.

An avid runner, Vicki often came to group wearing her running clothes and shoes. She was always the first person to arrive, full of energy and imbued with daunting willpower; Vicki modeled personal transformation as our group watched her blossom and change before our eyes. Her emotions ranged from fear to courage and her perceptions shifted from narrow-mindedness to receptivity. Never casting herself the victim, Vicki faced change as the warrior she had always been.

Vicki was one of the most successful of all of the participants in the classes I led. Her strength of character and willpower is what got her to stop running long enough to make a positive change.

The Transtheoretical Model

According to the work of James O. Prochaska, Ph.D. and other scientists, (see https://www.prochange.com/transtheoretical-model-of-behavior-change) change happens over time. The five stages of change have been identified as:

- Pre-contemplation
- Contemplation
- Preparation
- Action
- Maintenance and Relapse

Discussion of the Five Stages of Change

Write the five stages of change on a large Post-it® paper for the group to view and discuss according to these guidelines:

- **Pre-contemplation:** Unaware of the problem; no acknowledgement that a problem exists.
- **Contemplation:** Slight awareness of the problem; likely to be ambivalent about the need for change.
- **Preparation:** Ready to accept that there is a problem; intends to make a change.
- **Action:** Time and effort are committed to implement change.
- **Maintenance:** The person works to develop new behaviors and coping skills that become habits.

Ask the group what happens to them at the physical, emotional, and intellectual levels within each stage.

Words and/or Images about Change

For individual contemplation of life change, writing or drawing is necessary. Ask individuals to go within and find out where they stand with regard to their behaviors or ways of being that they would like to change.

Background music can be a powerful tool for people in contemplation of change. Here are some songs with the theme of change that may inspire action: https://danspira.com/2014/05/12/14-songs-about-change-a-trainers-personal-playlist/.

Tai Chi Energy

These exercises came from Capacitar.

The Rocking Movement: Stand with feet separated shoulder-width apart, hands at sides. Raise your heels and with palms facing upwards raise your hands to the level of your chest. Turn your palms downward and move your hands downward while you lower your heels and raise your toes in a rocking movement. Continue slowly rocking back and forth, breathing deeply. With each move, drop your shoulders, relax your arms and fingers. Do the exercise smoothly and slowly. Breathe deeply and imagine that your feet are planted securely on the earth. As you raise your hands, imagine you are bringing healing energy into your body to cleanse and fill your spirit.

This is a very beneficial movement for trauma and depression.

The Shower of Light: With left foot forward, raise your hands up over your head, and then move them downward as if showering yourself with light. Feel the energy cleansing and filling your being. Repeat on the right side, with right foot forward. Breathe in the shower of light, and then exhale and let go of any negativity within you. Feel the light cleansing and renewing you.

This is an excellent exercise for persons who are depressed or dealing with past wounds of trauma.

Let Go of the Past and Open to Receive: With left foot forward, palms curved softly downward, push your hands outward in a gentle arc, letting go of all tension, negativity, and violence within. Turn palms upward and draw them back towards the chest, breathing in peace and healing. Repeat with right foot forward. Breathe out the pain and violence. Breathe in peace and healing.

Heal, Healing, Healed

You don't get what you want, you get what you are.

~ DR. WAYNE DYER ~

Aims and Intentions
- Use traumas to engage healing
- Primitivo's story

Tools and/or Exercises
- Create a lotus flower as a representative of empowerment
- Compassionate listening exercise
- Emotional Freedom Technique

Materials
- An appropriate number of 10-inch square origami papers for the lotus project
- Link to origami tutorial: www.youtube.com/watch?v=Ig48H2G_oiU
- Pens or pencils and paper or journals
- Emotional Freedom Technique: https://capacitar.org/wp-content/uploads/EngCapEmergKit.pdf

To define "heal" and "healing," the Merriam-Webster online dictionary gives this: "heal: verb \'hēl \transitive verb 1 a: to make free from injury or disease : to make sound or whole *heal a wound* b: to make well again : to restore to health *heal the sick* 2 a : to cause (an undesirable condition) to be overcome : mend the troubles ... had not been forgotten, but they had been healed—William Power b : to patch up or correct (a breach or division) *heal a breach between friends* 3 : to restore to original purity or integrity *healed of sin* intransitive verb : to become free from injury or disease : to return to a sound state *The cut has already healed.* healed; healing : to make or become healthy or well again."

Everyone has their own definition of what "heal" means. Perhaps it is just one chapter, or a few. Maybe their entire book of life has been filled with traumas, as was the case for Primitivo.

Primitivo's Story

Primitivo was at the height of his addiction to crystal meth and was convinced his wife was sleeping with other men. In a large shed in his back yard, Primitivo constructed a cage. Inside the cage, he placed a mattress and some blankets, bowls for food and containers of water. The cage was constructed with his wife and daughter in mind. The day before the police arrived to arrest him, Primitivo had second thoughts and had taken the cage apart and disposed of it.

Crystal meth alters normal function in a specific part of the limbic system that processes emotions such as anger and fear. Because of this alteration, people using this drug can develop paranoid, aggressive, or violent states of mind.

Primitivo's father was an alcoholic. He and his sister often had to shelter themselves in their room to escape a beating. When they heard their father's truck in the driveway, they would peek out the window to see if he was sober or drunk. More than once Primitivo witnessed his mother being beaten by his father. When he was 7, while trying to protect her, he suffered a broken arm. It wasn't long after that when Primitivo began to drink alcohol.

In private, after one of our classes, Primitivo asked me if it would be OK for him to miss a week of group. He showed me a picture on his cell phone of one of his sons, who looked to be in his late 20s. This young man was living in Arizona after losing custody of his 2-year-old son. Primitivo's son had become a methamphetamine addict himself and was living in a drug den. Primitivo and his wife were going to get the son and bring him back home.

Primitivo was a year and seven months drug clean and sober the day he graduated from our group. It was our group's custom to celebrate each graduation with a meal, and we were busy setting up the tables. Primitivo asked if his wife, daughter, and son could stop in to say hello. Five minutes later, carrying 10 boxes of pizza, his wife, daughter, and now drug-free son walked into the room.

Primitivo's story shows an extreme example of healing and transformation. How does your own story of healing and transformation match with his?

Healing is an ongoing process. Think of a wound on your skin and the process it goes through before a scar forms. External healing from injury is observable; internal healing is unseen. Thus, it needs different tools and attention.

Go back to the Merriam-Webster Dictionary's definition of "healed" where it says: "to make or become healthy or well again." To be healed is to be "well again."

When Vincent J. Felitti, M.D. published his journal article in 2001 about the ACE study, he titled it "The Relationship of Adverse Childhood Experiences to Adult Health: Turning Gold into Lead." When a baby is born, it is perfect, like a piece of gold, but gold turns to lead if the baby endures trauma. When you have a goal of being healed, remember you will not return to a perfect state of wellness. There will always be a scar—possibly from one or more physical wounds, and definitely from emotional wounds. The point is to engage healing as an evolving process to keep the scars from re-opening.

Increased self-awareness leads to the development of self-management, which leads to personal empowerment. Personal empowerment recognizes the hurt in any active wound (physical or emotional), the healing process of the scab or "the psychological work," the permanence of a scar or a de-activated memory and the kintsukuroi that continues to shine a beautiful light—either internal or external.

Healing takes place when the metaphor of gold is applied to cracks of the damaged surface. The gold serves to cover the crack—but that does not mean the broken vessel is healed. The broken vessel is in a state of healing through the addition of gold.

Your goal as a human is to engage the process of healing but to reject the notion that you are healed, and thus have nothing more to do to maintain the health of your emotional and physical stability. Understanding that healing is a process keeps you in the "flow" of experience. This is the natural rhythm of life. The metaphor of the bicycle—wheeling toward and for healing—is important to keep in mind.

Lotus Flower

A lotus flower begins growing at the bottom of a muddy, murky pool and slowly emerges toward the surface, bursting out of the water into a beautiful blossom. During the night, the lotus closes and sinks under the water, then emerges again with the sunlight of a new day.

This lotus origami exercise requires the square of origami paper to become smaller and smaller. Therefore, it is easier to work with large pieces of origami paper. See the following YouTube video for a step-by-step tutorial: www.youtube.com/watch?v=Ig48H2G_oiU.

Here are some facts about the lotus plant to deliver while the class members are working on the origami creation exercise:

1. The lotus seeds contain perfectly formed leaves as miniatures of what they will become when it is time to bloom.

2. The lotus seed in the mud symbolizes the hardships and difficulties of life.

3. As with the stem growing toward the surface, people also grow through experiences, learning lessons along the way, removing obstacles, and overcoming adversities.

4. Just as the petals of the lotus flower unfold, people too unfold, and become like a lotus rising from murky waters and flowering into something beautiful.

5. The lotus seeds, containing perfectly formed leaves, symbolize human potential and resilience.

6. The symbol of the lotus is about never giving up, never quitting when things seem difficult.

7. The blossom of the lotus flower symbolizes enlightenment, awareness, and beauty.

Sharing the Lotus Experience

When the lotus origami exercise is completed, move into pairs, facing one another, and exchange your lotus flowers as a gift. Comment on the color, the experience of making it (degree of ease or difficulty), what you feel about the one you made and the one your partner made.

Explore or engage in a discussion using the following questions as prompts:

1. How are people like the lotus?
2. What were you like as a child?
3. What hardships did you face?
4. What have you learned from your hardships?
5. Do you know what you are here to accomplish in your life? If so, what is it?

Emotional Freedom Technique (EFT)

The Emotional Freedom Technique (EFT), developed by Gary Craig, Ph.D., is very useful for unblocking and healing strong emotions, fears, anxiety, emotional pain, anger, traumatic memories, phobias, and addictions, as well as for alleviating body symptoms of pain such as headaches and muscle pain. The technique is based on the energy field of body, mind, and emotions, along with the meridian theory of Eastern medicine. Problems, traumas, anxiety, and pain can cause blocks in a person's overall energy flow. Tapping on, or pressing acupressure points, that are connected with channels or meridians of energy can move blocked energy in congested areas and promote a healthy flow of energy throughout the body and in mental and emotional fields.

The following activity was adapted with permission from Gary Flint, Ph.D., creator of the Emotional Freedom Technique.

Choose to work with a problem, worry, phobia, anxiety, traumatic memory, or negative self-concept. Using a scale of 0—10, measure the level of anxiety that you feel when thinking about the issue. (0 means no anxiety, 10 means extremely high level of anxiety). If it is difficult to quantify or measure with a number, use a simple scale such as: none, small, medium, large; or, little to big; or, short to tall.

Holding the issue in your mind, practice EFT according to the instructions on the Capacitar EFT handout.

Nonviolence

When we judge others, we contribute to violence.

~ MARSHALL ROSENBERG ~

Aims and Intentions
- Understand nonviolent techniques to create healthy relationships that are supportive, trusting, warm and compassionate
- Wilma's story

Tools and/or Exercises
- Jackal and giraffe languages
- Words and/or images about emotions

Materials
- Language of the Heart/Language of the Giraffe link to information on the language of nonviolence: http://www.yesmagazine.org/issues/rx-for-the-earth/837
- Pens or pencils and paper or journals

Dr. Marshall Rosenberg, Ph.D., founder of an international nonprofit, the Center for Nonviolent Communication, coined two types of language: jackal and giraffe. The term "giraffe language" means nonviolent communication. Dr. Rosenberg chose the giraffe because it has the largest heart of all land animals (a giraffe heart may weigh up to 40 pounds), and this unique animal has a broad, wide view of all things in its landscape. He felt that "giraffe language" is the heart's language.

But most cultures teach people to speak the language of the jackal, which is through demands that provoke defensiveness, resistance, and counterattack.

Jackals, due to their low proximity to the ground, tend to see just what's under their noses. Jackal language symbolizes narrow, self-protecting, limited communication.

In contrast, the language of giraffe is one of requests. It allows people to communicate in respectful, compassionate ways. The benefit of giraffe language in relationships is that it avoids assumptions and tries to clarify feelings. The giraffe creates harmony instead of discord. The benefits of using giraffe language become apparent quickly, and you'll want to make a habit of using it. See an interview with Marshall Rosenberg and get examples of jackal and giraffe language here: http://www.yesmagazine.org/issues/rx-for-the-earth/837.

Being raised in what appeared to be a loving environment did not guarantee that Wilma was trauma-free.

Wilma's Story

Married in her early twenties to her high school sweetheart, Wilma was full of hope and expectations. She knew that her husband drank but she thought that once married he would spend less time with friends and more time at home. Two years into their marriage, when Wilma gave birth to a baby girl, the stakes heightened for her. The wellbeing of her daughter's safety and security made her question the marriage.

Her husband had not changed. Wilma found him to be less than the man she thought he was or wanted him to be. In her eyes, he lacked purpose and drive. She grew tired of trying to encourage him to strive for a better job. Wilma was resentful; she felt him to be immature and unmotivated. She filed for divorce.

Two years later Wilma married a man who was driven and successful but also very jealous, possessive, and verbally abusive. One day, not able to take it anymore, Wilma struck him with a ceramic bowl. He called the police and Wilma was arrested.

Deciding that the second marriage was over, Wilma rented a one-bedroom apartment in a complex near her second ex-husband so that her daughter could maintain a relationship with her stepdad. Since her daughter was only a year old when Wilma's first marriage ended, the stepdad was the only father her daughter knew.

Having been raised in a loving family, Wilma couldn't understand why she had such bad luck with men. Her father had been a good provider; a loving and caring man. But as she spoke about him, it became clear that her father had an authoritarian personality. The stories Wilma shared painted the picture of how she'd grown up in an environment where absolute obedience and submission to her father was expected.

As Wilma shared yet another story of having to call the police because of neighbors fighting, she broke down. Stories shared by all the women in the group at that moment made Wilma realize that her lifestyle and where she lived was not good for her daughter. She told us that she needed to form a new life. She was getting to know herself, learning to care for and love herself, so that she could be a good role model for her daughter.

Overcoming the kind of trauma Wilma suffered meant that she had to pass through an exposure to violence to realize she did not need a man in her life. Her movement toward nonviolence allowed her to find trust in herself, and to build skills that took her from cleaning houses to working as a nutritionist.

Jackal and Giraffe Languages

Use a Post-it® tablet sheet to create and post the following chart for a group discussion:

Dominant Paradigm	Nonviolent Paradigm
Jackal	Giraffe
Judgment	Observation
Evaluation	Feelings
Behavior	Needs
Obedience	Connection
Conditional	Unconditional

Ask the group the following six questions, or, divide into pairs for one-on-one discussions:

1. Do you believe that your emotional responses were modeled and sculpted since childhood by your parents or caretakers?

2. Do you believe that health and wellbeing is not about erasing old beliefs, associations, or ways of being, but it is about building new ways of thinking and being?

3. Why do you think your parents or caregivers acted the way they did during your childhood?

4. What would you like your children to learn in being parented by you? If you could ask them at the age of 25 what they learned from you, they would say…?

5. Where do you see yourself at this time—as a jackal or a giraffe?

6. What do you want to change now that you've learned about the languages of the jackal and the giraffe?

Words and/or Images about Emotions

After the group discussion or pair share, use the following prompts to write or draw:

1. How easy is it for you to forgive those who have caused you pain?
2. What is the dominant emotion in your life right now?
3. What three things do you wish for yourself?

If you have children, what three things do you wish for them?

Creativity as a Path to Self-Awareness

Poetry is when an emotion has found its thought and the thought has found words.

~ ROBERT FROST ~

Aims and Intentions
* Poetry as a means of deconstructing and examining life
* Hildalgo's story

Tools and/or Exercises
* Poem by Thich Nhat Hanh: "Please Call Me by My True Names"
* Mindful walking exercise
* Words and/or images about poetry, and identity or compassion
* Intergenerational poetry

Materials
* Link to the poem: "Please Call Me by My True Names," www.youtube.com/watch?v=hbb34ujv6xg
* Walking meditation video: www.youtube.com/watch?v=YSOKte6TeMI
* Pens or pencils and paper or journals

The art of poetry defies definition, but Emily Dickinson wrote: "If I feel physically as if the top of my head were taken off, I know that is poetry." Many people have felt so moved by reading or hearing poetry, and thus it can be considered a tool as well as an art. Think of some other great poets and their value to society. Poetry is about the power and beauty of words to represent deep concepts and philosophy. "Please Call Me by My True Names" is one such poem. Written by Thich Nhat Hanh, a Vietnamese Buddhist monk, peace activist, and author of several books that contain great wisdom (especially his book titled *Anger*), it is a poem about the power of forgiveness, love, and acceptance.

Hidalgo's Story

Hidalgo brought to life for our group what the loss of a father, and a war, can do to a child and how these experiences shape the man. It's one thing to know, as we now do, that the absence of a father (incarceration, death, separation, or divorce) has adverse physical and behavioral consequences for a growing child. It's another to see and hear the stories of such a life.

Hidalgo's memories of the first six years of his childhood in El Salvador were lovely ones. The family was not rich, but they were happy and never lacked for anything. His father, who he remembers to have always been a hard worker, owned a small farm. They had a couple of sheep, plenty of chickens, and a cow—the land and animals provided all Hidalgo's family needed.

But then the war came and life was forever changed.

Hidalgo was tall, lean, well-muscled, and a man of few words. When he spoke, we sat up and listened. It was easy to believe that during his three-year prison stint he was asked to become an enforcer, a request he refused because he didn't believe in hurting someone who had done nothing to him.

As our time together in group went on, Hidalgo's stories got more personal and it became evident that his need to tell them gave him a chance to free himself of the internal demons he'd carried for so long.

He spoke of cheerful walks home from the fields after a hard day's work, following the smell of his mother's cooking. His walk home was dreaded once the war began. The cemetery he crossed on the way to and from home became a dumping ground of unburied dead bodies; the ones killed by both the army and guerrillas.

It was during one of these dread-filled walks with his father and brother that Hidalgo's life was forever changed. A truck of soldiers pulled up alongside them, and at gunpoint they forced his brother and father into the back of the truck. Hidalgo screamed and cried so much and so hard that they released him and his brother, but the two never saw their father again. Hidalgo's heart hardened and he began to feel hate.

The trauma of war and unspeakable violence he witnessed hardened Hidalgo's heart, and the harder his heart became, the more protected he felt. In our class, Hidalgo went through the hand-washing exercise that is found in the book *You, and You in Relationship*. Like the experience of Emily Dickinson, the washing of Hidalgo's hands gave him the power of poetry.

Poetry has a way of bleeding through the cracks, seeping in, and shining its light.

"Please Call Me by My True Names"

Listen to the poem aloud all the way through via this link: www.youtube.com/watch?v=hbb34ujv6xg. Listen to it again a second time and write down a word, line, or lines that have meaning for you. While listening to it a third time, reflect on the meaning and contemplate the value of its message in your life.

Discussion of "Please Call Me by My True Names"

After listening to the poem three times, enter a group discussion using the following questions as prompts:

1. What line (or lines) speaks to you most? Why?
2. What roles have you played?
3. How deep is your joy?
4. How deep is your pain?
5. Are you the person in power or the laborer paying a "debt of blood?"

Words and/or Images about Identity or Compassion

Next, draw a picture or write a poem regarding the topic of identity or the practice of compassion.

Intergenerational Poetry

Many people have an intuitive sense that poetry can be healing. I am one of those people. Finding the words to articulate a traumatic experience can bring relief. Poetry serves as the canvas where those words are painted. We live in a culture where many subjects are considered taboo. Poetry gives ways to talk about them.

My father was a poet, but only on rare occasions in his life did he share this side of himself. After his death, I came across a folder of poems he wrote. The poem below, "Estranged Memories," was one that arrived in me while I was walking on the beach. It is a conversation between the spirit of me, my father, Leonard Cohen, and God. I took some of the words my father wrote and intermingled them with my own. Doing this allowed me to experience my father in a new way.

I like this quote by Dan Siegel, M.D.: "To appreciate the benefits of interrelations you simply have to open your mind." If you open your heart as well, you transcend space and time to touch moments of grace.

Estranged Memories

Over a calm sea,
on this day
estranged memories
arise.

Did I ever
love you?

To these thoughts
the silence chatters
during my stride
through
placid sunrise.

Did I ever
hurt you?

Sand beneath
my restless feet
echoes cries of
yesteryear.

Discard, forsake,
or desert you?

Scattered feelings
breathe inside
a wounded
hurt and
broken heart.

"Why
couldn't
you
love
me?"

Is it mercy
that I seek?
Love—unconditional?
Compassion?
These questions
give me
choice to speak.

Why did
you hurt
me?

Don't explain
or apologize.
The veil
remains
over our eyes.

From
silence

undaunted
memories shine
through the cracks.
From beyond the sea
a quiet,
mournful,
merciful cry.

My wish:
I want to have been
the father you
ought to have
had.

In wish
is motion
and hope.
A transitory,
perhaps
permanent,
reprise.

If the group is willing to do so, encourage sharing of poems or drawings.

Mindful Walking

Read aloud this quote by Thich Nhat Hanh: "We have to walk in a way that we only print peace and serenity on the Earth. Walk as if you are kissing the Earth with your feet." Then watch this video about mindful walking: www.youtube.com/watch?v=YSOKte6TeMI.

Make time to walk and breathe around the room, as instructed by the video. Take note of what feelings arise as you walk.

The Five C Words

*Communication leads to community, that is,
to understanding, intimacy and mutual valuing.*

~ ROLLO MAY ~

Aims and Intentions
* Learn the five C Words: Calm, Compassion, Connection, Competence, Clarity
* Destiny's story

Tools and/or Exercises
* Write the five C words to develop definitions in group discussion
* Role play exercise

Materials
* Post-it® large tablet and a Sharpie® marker

The five C Words give great benefits to people when they know them and put them into practice. Write the words and post them to hold a group discussion regarding their meanings. Here are the words and some guidelines:

Calm The brain learns best when the body is in a physiological state of equilibrium: calm and relaxed, yet engaged and alert. Mindfulness practice and resonant connections with others allow a person to rest steady in a state of equilibrium.

Compassion Mindfulness and empathy keep the mind and heart open in times of confusion, suffering, and sorrow. Mindfulness allows a person to engage with what needs to be addressed in the moment. Compassion allows people to analyze and come to terms with what happened:

a. This is what happened.

b. This is what I did to survive.

c. This has been the cost of endurance.

d. This is what I learned.

e. This is how I can respond and be resilient now.

Connections Clarity about options includes connecting to the places of safety and resources that are the foundations of skillful coping—people, places and practices that support being responsive and resilient. When a person anchors in the resource of their true nature as their true home or point of reference, they remain open to the "plane of open possibilities" and new solutions to old problems. The insights from this plane inform the person's view of the capacities of self and choices of actions.

Competence Wise effort is essential to the skillful alleviation of suffering. Mindfulness and learning from others as role models allow individuals to "crack the code," to discern wholesome from unwholesome, to perceive and let go of past trauma, to cultivate qualities of loving kindness, compassion, generosity, gratitude, blamelessness and awe that broaden and build resources in the immediate future as well as long-term.

Clarity Steady, non-judgmental awareness of experience through the true self leads to mental and heart-centered clarity. Clarity allows a person to see what is happening then respond to triggers and traumas with open-mindedness. It leads to being able to choose what needs to change, and then to make change, with far more flexibility.

In this story, about a mother and a daughter, the five C words are demonstrated in a single evening.

Destiny's Story

Destiny loves her very shy 18-year-old daughter. We know this because Destiny told it to our group. Shyness is a trait the mother and daughter share, but over the course of the year the group members watched Destiny's personality emerge.

In the beginning Destiny barely spoke. When she did, her voice was barely audible. She'd learned to hold in all of her needs, thoughts, and feelings, and to reveal very little about her life. On the day she told us about a dance her daughter had been invited to, you could have heard a pin drop.

Destiny agonized over the decision but in the end decided to let her daughter go because it was the first time she was ever asked to attend any event, let alone a dance. Knowing her daughter really liked the boy who'd asked her lessened Destiny's worry.

What Destiny was most proud to share was how she dealt with her thoughts and feelings upon visiting with the young man who picked up and then delivered her daughter back home. The moment she opened the door, Destiny immediately found herself judging her daughter's date in the same way her mother had judged every guy Destiny had ever dated. Her internal dialogue went something like this, "He's not that handsome," and, "Definitely not good enough for my daughter," and, "Those clothes make him look like a gang member." When he handed Destiny the flowers he'd brought to her it took everything she had to say, "Thank you."

Destiny suffered and obsessed the whole night, while a battle raged in her head over the desire to tell her daughter everything she'd felt about the boy. Instead, seeing the happiness that radiated from her daughter's face when she came home, Destiny bit her lip, held in her thoughts, and drew blood in order to keep to herself the words she knew would ruin her daughter's memories of a beautiful night. As she watched her daughter make her way to her room with a bounce in her step, tears ran down Destiny's face. She wasn't crying out of frustration for not having said what she'd felt about the boy, but for all the times her own mother, unable to bite her tongue, used her words to belittle, demean, and shame her.

Calm. Compassion. Connection. Competence. Clarity. What Destiny and her daughter experienced in this evening led both of them out of judgment and into love.

Role Play

This exercise brings back the giraffe and jackal languages. Form pairs and have each pair decide who plays the role of jackal and who plays giraffe. Go through the five C words and come up with a scenario, perhaps similar to Destiny's story, to play out. Alternatively, use your imagination to develop a scene like the ones below:

- Someone blames you falsely for a problem
- Someone calls you names
- Someone takes something that belongs to you
- Someone abuses your friend
- Someone demeans you due to your sexual orientation
- Someone demeans you because of your income level
- Someone asks for something you are not able or willing to give

How would the jackal deal in one of those scenarios? The giraffe? Take at least 15 minutes to come up with the script. If time permits, have each pair present their skit to the rest of the group.

Culture and Implicit Bias

*A people without the knowledge of their past history,
origin and culture is like a tree without roots.*

~ MARCUS GARVEY ~

Aims and Intentions
* Understand that a person's culture (race, socio-economic situation) is one of the factors that informs and create their world view
* Learn the concept of implicit bias using the Implicit Association Test (IAT)
* John's story

Tools and/or Exercises
* Take the Implicit Association Test
* Words and/or images exercise about bias

Materials
* Link to IAT: https://implicit.harvard.edu/implicit/takeatest.html.
* Pens or pencils and paper or journals
* Post-it® large tablet and Sharpie® marker

The Implicit Association Test (IAT) was developed at Harvard University to measure attitudes and beliefs that people may be unwilling or unable to report. Your IAT results may show that you have an implicit attitude of which you were unaware. Find information about the IAT here: https://implicit.harvard.edu/implicit/takeatest.html. This link will take you to the preliminary information page. In order to take any of the tests you must click on the link at the bottom of the page.

It is important to know about this test, even if it is not possible for the class to take it. The following story told by John illustrates the idea of implicit association.

John's Story

Abandoned by his family at the age of 14 for being bisexual, John aged out of the foster care system at 18 and spent the majority of his young adulthood living in shelters, on the streets, or sleeping on people's couches. During his time in our group, he was living out of a minivan bought with money earned working at a pet shop. He told us he'd worked there for five years, the longest job he'd ever held. The owner was more a mother to him than his own mother ever was. She constantly praised and validated him, often telling him that he was the best dog groomer she'd ever hired.

One day, a male customer complained about the grooming John had given his dog and John got so angry that he went to the cash register, grabbed the amount of money the customer had paid and threw the money at him. John then went outside but the customer followed him and a shoving match ensued. The altercation ended with John hitting the customer.

His boss could no longer handle John's temper and outbursts of rage. She cried the day she let him go, but John knew she had no choice.

John loved animals more than people, especially dogs. They never made him angry and never let him down. His love for them was so evident that the men in our group often told him he should start his own pet grooming business. In fact, many of them gave John a night on a soft couch and a meal in exchange for dog grooming services.

The group members liked John and accepted him for who he was.

Implicit bias is "tested" by everyone, every day. The people who witnessed John's situation knew that a wounded human, just like a wounded animal, is dangerous. However, when time is spent on listening to a person's story, implicit bias softens its hard edges and leads to the kind of openhearted treatment John was given.

About Implicit Bias

Reflect on how you learned to define yourself by your family and culture. This is called "acculturation" and it is longstanding, or "rooted," energy that is a remnant from your past generations. In Chapter 1 of *Wheeling to Healing: Broken Heart on a Bicycle*, I've given insight into my own acculturation:

> *Lake Titicaca is home to one of the world's largest frogs, the Titicaca frog. An endangered species, it faces the possibility of becoming extinct. But that was not the case in the 1970s, when the famous explorer and conservationist Jacques Cousteau, then searching Lake Titicaca for Inca treasure, reported seeing thousands of these frogs, some almost 20 inches long.*
>
> *My father's father, Sebastian, once told me that the native people believed these frogs had special powers, particularly the power to bring rain. He told me a tale in which the Aymara Indians captured and carried the frogs in ceramic pots to a hillside where the frogs would call in distress. The people thought the frogs' calls sounded to the gods like a plea for rain. Once the downpour began, the pots overflowed and the sacred animals escaped back to the lake.*
>
> *The frogs in my grandfather's story were one thing, but a real distress call was going on—and it was coming from me. Often, as a child, I cried out to God in prayer from the darkness of my bedroom, imploring Him to stop my father from hurting my mother.*
>
> *In fact, the trauma in my childhood began before I even learned to pray.*

Implicit Association Test

Choose an area you want to explore and take one of the IATs available for that area. Once you have taken the test(s), write or draw your insights you gained, especially the ones that you were not aware of in a conscious way.

Once each group member has completed the tests, gather in a circle and share thoughts, insights, and feelings about acculturation, bias, and how people carry the beliefs of their parents, grandparents, and ancestors.

Words and/or Images about Bias

Explore answers to the following six questions through writing or drawing:

1. Did your IAT results surprise you?
2. Do you feel your results were accurate?
3. Did you pick a bias you expected to do well with?
4. What insights were reinforced by taking the test?
5. How can what you learned through the IAT results help you to reflect on your own biases before you choose to interpret, challenge, or ignore the messages you receive from others?

How can you own and not hide from your biases?

Two Tasks, Two Masks

Seven times have I despised my soul: The sixth time when she despised the ugliness of a face, and knew not that it was one of her own masks.

~ KAHLIL GIBRAN ~

Aims and Intentions
* Understand the "two tasks" and how they relate to "two masks"
* Erica's story

Tools and/or Exercises
* Gender roles and contrasts
* Poem by Nancy R. Smith: "For Every Woman"
* Stages of the Ethic of Care
* Create a mask

Materials
* Link to Carol Gilligan's Stages of the Ethic of Care, http://humangrowth.tripod.com/id2.html
* Link to the poem, "For Every Woman": www.youtube.com/watch?v=DiH0OTS_Uis
* Mask-making materials: plastic gallon jugs and papier-mâché recipe: https://www.youtube.com/watch?v=FCiYNE_hmNg

Franciscan priest, writer, speaker and teacher, Father Richard Rohr says that there are two tasks life assigns to every individual: "The first task is to build a strong container or 'identity' and the second task is to find the contents that the container was meant to hold." What happens when you let society determine your container?

Erica knew.

Erica's Story

A conflict with her 17-year-old stepson resulted in Erica spending a week in jail. Her stepson was removed from their home and remanded into a juvenile detention facility. That fight, one of many, escalated from verbal sparring up to Erica being shoved to the ground by the stepson. She picked herself up, took a kitchen knife, and cut him on the arm he'd raised in self-protection.

Raised in a traditional Mexican home, Erica was taught that the man was head of the family and a woman's job was to cook, clean, and take care of the house. Erica was much closer in age to her stepson than to her husband, a man 33 years her senior, and she expected her husband to discipline his son and make his son respect her. In her eyes, the boy was lazy and spoiled. She was tired of caring for him on a daily basis, a task made even less appealing by bouts of morning sickness.

In our group meetings, Erica often wondered out loud if her husband would love the child she was carrying as much as he loved his son. She was going to have a girl, and the culture into which Erica was born taught her that boys were prized; girls were lesser. Erica had seen the disappointment in her husband's eyes when the doctor had given them the news.

Society, and her baby's father, gave Erica a mask she did not want. Her task was to face resentment and fear. When she took ownership and responsibility of herself, her thoughts, and stopped judging the man who represented the mask, she engaged in a healing process that would be passed on to her child.

Your experiences shape the mask you wear in public. Yet, every individual has the power to re-create that mask if they can shift their attitudes and fulfill their life's purpose. By recognizing and owning this power, you can build with it to discover and live your life purpose with more joy, love, and wisdom. Your mask becomes a symbol of your inherent truth, goodness, and beauty.

By creating a mask for yourself you'll explore your persona. The word 'persona' comes from the Latin word for mask. Persona refers to the practical and successful personality that people use most of the time in social relationships.

It's a facade that develops in childhood when you get approval, or disapproval, for behaving in certain ways. For example, you learn to disguise and repress whatever behavior is not approved—emotions like anger, greed, envy, and jealousy. You may also repress good aspects such as creativity or self-confidence if these qualities are not appreciated or affirmed.

Gender Roles and Contrasts

Your gender identity is the most intimate, yet one of the most visible ways, that you show up for other people. Why does it have to be like this? That's a rhetorical question, but it relates to the human need for contrasts. Of the many ways to gender identify, all categories play off the two main ones: male and female. Those two were the only 'accepted' gender roles in many cultures and for many centuries. Those boundaries are in the process of going away so that people can explore the meaning of duality and contrast, and find answers for dealing with gender identity in ways that are open-minded and loving.

"For Every Woman" poem by Nancy R. Smith

Listen to "For Every Woman" on YouTube: www.youtube.com/watch?v=Di-H0OTS_Uis. Follow this three-stage process: 1. Listen to it be read it aloud. 2. Listen again for words or phrases that speak to you. 3. Listen again and reflect on what the poem makes you feel and how it informs you.

After studying the poem, ask the following five questions for group discussion:

1. Is it true that when one person is limited by either belief or expectation, everyone is limited?
2. When one person usurps power over someone else, or makes up a rule, should it be questioned as to whether or not it is fair?
3. Why has the female been considered weak, stupid, not in control of her emotions, and her work not valued?
4. Does the poet show how the roles that identify limit both female and male gender?
5. Do all gender identifications require limits?

Gender relevance, at its most basic point of meaning, is about how a species reproduces itself. Gender has been described, translated, marketed to, usurped, criticized and distorted in so many ways other than the use for which it was intended: reproduction. Animal bodies are designed to reproduce. Reproduction is to be respected as such. Does it make a difference to you to discover this and does it allow you to peel back some of the layers gender identity has collected over the years?

Stages of the Ethic of Care

Find information on the "Stages of the Ethic of Care" by Carol Gilligan at http://humangrowth.tripod.com/id2.html and discuss the chart that shows the stages.

Gilligan shows that men and women develop through three stages of hierarchy. She makes the point that both genders do so in a different way: Men develop through the moral hierarchy using the logic of rights and justice; women develop through the same moral hierarchy using the logic of care and relationship. The three stages of hierarchy are:

Pre-Conventional (selfish or egocentric): This is when the person cares only for the self in order to ensure survival. This is how everyone acts when they are children. In this phase, the person's attitude is considered selfish, even though the person sees a connection between themselves and others.

Conventional (care or ethnocentric): This is when selfishness transitions to responsibility to others. More care is shown for other people. Gilligan says this is apparent in the roles of mother and wife. In this phase, there is a tension between responsibility of caring for others and caring for self.

Post Conventional (universal care or world centric): In this phase, a person transitions from just being good to the truth that she is a person too. Acceptance of the principal of care for self and then others is shown. Many people never reach this level.

Create a Mask

Simple mask making steps are found in the section titled "Recognizing Loss and the Process of Grief," above. Here again is the recipe for papier-mâché: https://www.youtube.com/watch?v=FCiYNE_hmNg.

During this hands-on activity, ask: "How does healthy attachment influence the mask you wear?" Then, ask the participants to reflect on the following quotes as you read the following aloud and ask them to reflect as they work:

> **From André Berthiaume:** *"We all wear masks, and the time comes when we cannot remove them without removing some of our own skin."*

> **From Father Richard Rohr:** *"Basically if you get mirrored well early in life, you do not have to spend the rest of your life looking in Narcissus's mirror or begging for the attention of others."*

From Christopher Barzak: *"Nothing is more real than the masks we make to show each other who we are."*

After the group has created their mask forms, they need to be left to dry or set for the next group meeting.

Creating a New Mask

*Each night, when I go to sleep, I die.
And the next morning, when I wake up, I am reborn.*

~ MAHATMA GANDHI ~

Aims and Intentions
- Who are you and how do you present yourself to the world?
- Malcolm's story

Tools and/or Exercises
- New mask exercise
- Word and/or images exercise about masks

Materials
- Paints and objects brought by group members for decorating the mask forms
- Pens or pencils and paper or journals
- Music player with meditative/contemplative music selections

Like healing, understanding the relationship between who you are and how you present yourself to the world happens as a process. Adapting to a certain occasion, behaving in a manner suitable to that occasion, and knowing how best to navigate the multitude of expectations others may have about you are the keys to living a good life. This is not something people learn in school; they learn it moment-by-moment. So, having created a mask (and now decorating it) as a reflection of what's inside is an important exercise.

The mask that Malcolm wore could not cover the extent of his emotional wounds.

Malcolm's Story

One month after his attempted suicide, Malcolm woke up in a hospital. He'd been put into a medically induced coma to save his life. Throughout our first six months together, our group listened to the rancor and bitterness that emanated from him anytime he spoke of his wife. Although she'd left him three months prior to his suicide attempt, he found it hard to forgive her for never once visiting him in the hospital. He was obsessed with her and what he saw as her faults and failings.

His turning point came with the introduction of the concepts of mindfulness and meditation. These simple tools changed him and freed him from his former self.

During our group meditations, Malcolm sat in a chair with his hands resting on his knees, eyes closed tight as he entered into deep concentration to focus on himself.

While wearing his mask, Malcolm could not figure out how to forgive himself or his wife. When his mask came off, he engaged in meditation as a method of self-improvement, and we saw the way he experienced freedom without having to wear a mask any longer.

A New Mask

The masks made in the last meeting are ready to be painted and decorated. During time spent on completion of the mask, play contemplative or meditative background music and ask that the participants refrain from conversation, but while they work, ask them to think about their own answers to the following 14 questions:

1. What are you afraid of and what are you doing to overcome it?

2. What is something you would like to change about yourself and why?

3. What is one personality trait you share with your parents?
4. Who or what makes you happy?
5. What is important to you?
6. Was there a time when you made someone else feel sad?
7. What is your favorite thing to do with your free time?
8. What are you good at?
9. Why is your best friend your best friend?
10. Was there a time when you laughed with complete freedom?
11. How has making your mask helped you to reflect on your life journey?
12. Has making your mask improved your sense of self?
13. Are you more aware of the positive qualities you embody at this point in your life?
14. Are there any characteristics you would like to acquire, or to change for the better, within yourself?

Words and/or Images about Masks

As the decorations on the masks dry, write or draw about the mask creation experience. What has it made you feel, remember, understand, and encounter?

Trauma and Theater

Living is strife and torment, disappointment and love and sacrifice, golden sunsets and black storms. I said that some time ago, and today I do not think I would add one word.

~ LAURENCE OLIVIER ~

Aims and Intentions
- Use theater techniques for freedom to tell your stories
- Connect your story with those of others
- Ava's story

Tools and/or Exercises
- Choosing and reading monologues
- Guided meditation
- Monologue and meditation words and/or images exercise

Materials
- Library books that contain Shakespearean, Greek, or contemporary monologues or access this or other websites for materials: https://monologueblogger.com/contemporary-monologues-from-plays-and-stand-alone/

The ability to act is like the ability to draw—anyone can do it with a bit of coaching. Theater (as in 'acting') is intuitive. It helps people acquire, exercise, and build the quality of empathy. It also allows for a deeper level of self-exploration. Individuals who have been traumatized learn to fear being seen, or they lose touch with their feelings and tend to not let others get close to them. Theatrical monologues allow people to develop a relationship with the self, access emotions, and explore other avenues of engaging with the world.

Ava's story demonstrates the kind of drama that rises out of everyday life, when tension builds, and an event must occur in order to achieve resolution.

Ava's Story

Tough-as nails with a heart of gold would be the appropriate and best way to describe Ava. The youngest of seven and the only girl, Ava grew up constantly competing with her brothers and discovered that she was just as capable of doing anything a boy could do. She also realized that if you wanted something badly enough you had to fight for it. The one thing she never had to fight for was her mother's love. Being the only girl it was destined that she and her mom would be especially close.

At age 22, seeking economic security, and fleeing war, Ava and her husband left Nicaragua for the United States to find work. They left their infant son with Ava's mother. For three years they worked hard; Ava cleaned homes and her husband was a day laborer. Like many immigrants, they sent much of what they earned home to help their families. What they didn't spend on the basics, they saved. When they had enough money, Ava and her husband went home to retrieve their son.

Once back in the United States, Ava decided to enroll in cosmetology school part time. This decision did not sit well with her husband but she was not deterred and in fact, it made her bold. She asked her mother to come care for her grandson while Ava worked and went to school.

A bold wife, unresolved PTSD from living through war, and his mother-in-law's presence in the home created tension for Ava's husband. One night during an argument after dinner, he pushed Ava and she fell. At first she was in shock because he had never been violent toward her, but once Ava heard her son's screams and saw her mom's tears she picked up the hammer her husband had used to put up their kitchen cabinets and threw it at him. The hammer glanced off his head and drew a lot of blood. Their screams caused the neighbors to call the police and when they arrived on the scene, they determined Ava was the aggressor. She was arrested and taken to jail, then assigned to our group to learn how to deal with her aggressive impulses and anger.

Life was a stage for Ava as she watched from the front row and then decided to join her oppressors on that stage. While in our group, Ava moved away from the drama of an unloving marriage and started a new life, out of the need for a shadow of self-protection.

Choosing and Reading Monologues

Acting requires making a connection first with self, then with the 'other.' Involving group members in monologue work enables them to explore emotions in new ways. They learn to name and encounter different emotional experiences in a safe, controlled manner. The choice to accept one of many different emotions to portray in a controlled environment develops the ability to empathize.

Here is a list of titles of monologues to use with the group: https://monologueblogger.com/contemporary-monologues-from-plays-and-stand-alone/.

Each participant chooses a short monologue to read aloud as a story. For the second reading, add feelings, voice inflections, or other embellishments. After everyone has finished the second reading, prepare the group for a guided meditation.

Guided Meditation

Close your eyes, taking a number of deep breaths. When ready, allow yourself to go to what you consider a safe place, a place where you have felt safe and at peace; perhaps a comfortable, safe room or a place outdoors in nature.

Take time to get a sense of being in that place in your mind and body. Feel the atmosphere of that place with all your senses. Without opening your eyes, look around your safe place. What do you see?

Give a few minutes for them to soak in the surroundings.

Now, look into the distance and see coming towards you a person who has made you feel safe, happy, and strong. Spend time with this person and really see them.

Share with them a memory of a difficult or troubling moment you had and have kept as a secret—something you alone have had to carry all this time. As you sit or stand in that safe place with the person who cares about you, become aware that in sharing your secret you no longer have to carry it alone.

How does it feel to let it go?

Does it make you feel lighter?

Does it make you feel free?

Sit or stand with the feelings. Feel a weight lift from your heart.

Now thank the person who appeared to you and tell them that it's time for them go back from wherever they came. Say goodbye and watch them leave with the secret you no longer have to carry.

Take your time allowing yourself to return to the present.

When you're ready, open your eyes and look at the monologue on which you are working. While sitting with the feelings brought up by the guided meditation, read the monologue to yourself once again and allow what you are feeling to inform the words.

Monologue and Meditation Reflections

Reflect on five questions about these two experiences by writing or drawing:

1. Was there any change each time the piece was read?
2. Did you or those watching notice any change in your body or your voice?
3. Were you more or less present?
4. What emotions did you feel?

Did you have any surprises?

Role Play Mirror and True Self Mirror

Love is our true destiny. We do not find the meaning of life by ourselves alone—we find it with another.

~ THOMAS MERTON ~

Aims and Intentions
* Understand the differences between 'soul' and 'spirit' and the connections between body, mind, spirit of being, and soul
* The concept of mirror neurons
* Elmer's story

Tools and/or Exercises
* Interactive mirror exercise
* Individual mirror exercise
* Words and/or images about witness

Materials
* Capacitar exercise link: www.capacitar.org/wp-content/uploads/EngCapEmergKit.pdf
* Hand-held mirror
* Pens or pencils and paper or journals

Mirroring the action of another person allows you to have empathy. I read *Mirroring People: The Science of Empathy and How We Connect with Others,* by

Marco Iacoboni, M.D., Ph.D., and was especially intrigued by how he described empathy in chapter four. I reached out in 2013 to request a meeting with him; he invited me to come to UCLA and sit in on a session on brain mapping. I attended the seminar and afterwards, he invited me to his office.

He spoke to me of how mirror neurons teach us to be human. For example, when I look at you performing an action, if I can activate the part of my brain that I use for the same action, I don't have to figure out what you're doing. There's an immediate understanding that's made possible through mirror neuron cells. Mirror neurons exist in everyone's brain and allow for connection, empathy, and love. Dr. Iacoboni taught me that we are all interconnected at a basic, pre-reflective level and are wired for empathy.

Standing with Elmer as he faced the metaphor of his mirror were three men he remembered as being forces in his life—two negative, one positive. In real life, the three men never met, except in Elmer's memory.

Elmer's Story

Two important men marched in and out of Elmer's life by the time he was 14. The first was his father who abandoned him and his sisters when he was 2. The second was an alcoholic drug addict who physically abused his mom and was mean to all of them.

Fortunately for Elmer, there was a third man who became his stepfather. For the first time in his life, Elmer felt genuinely cared for, validated, and supported. When Elmer came home at 15 with news that his 14-year-old girlfriend was pregnant, the stepfather brought the families together and got them to pledge to help care for the baby so that Elmer and his girlfriend could finish school.

This stepfather became Elmer's mentor, role model, and confidant.

Elmer told our group that he would never forget the day that his stepfather came home and asked everyone into the kitchen. Elmer was out back in the yard playing catch with his 5-year old son. He picked up his boy, carried him into the kitchen, and sat with his son on his lap. Elmer and his family heard that the stepfather had been diagnosed with bladder cancer, and it had spread all over his body. Elmer cradled his little boy into his chest and wept while his stepfather stood at his side, stroking his head.

The man who became Elmer's stepfather modeled for him the way Elmer wanted to be. The love shown to Elmer by his stepfather led to a deep connection with his own son. When Elmer and his son look into a mirror together, both will have a sense of the reflection of the stepfather.

Interactive Mirror

This exercise is to show how the body's five senses and four elements (physical, spirit, soul, intellect/mind) come together as illustrated when the selected group members enact dialogue and follow direction provided by the Actor and the Witness. Helpful tool: For more information, see Bessel Van Der Kolk's book, *The Body Keeps the Score*, the chapter titled, "Revising the Past."

Two people volunteer to sit in the center of the group. One will play a role as the Actor, the other as the Witness. The Witness is an accepting, nonjudgmental participant who observes the Actor and mirrors his or her emotional state. The Actor expresses a thought or emotion to the Witness who, in turn, takes notice and echoes what they've received from the Actor. The Witness will mirror the inner tension the Actor reveals.

Here is an example:

Actor: *I can't feel anything in my body and my mind is blank.*

Witness: *I can see how worried you are that your mind is blank and you don't feel anything.*

Actor: *That's right.*

Witness: *Then tell us a story about something going on in your life right now. Please bring your story to life by selecting members from this group to role-play with you.*

The Actor selects other group members to play roles from the story he articulates.

Individual Mirror

After the role-playing exercise has gone a few rounds with different people, pass around a hand-held mirror (or several if you have them) that is large enough for a person to see his or her face as completely as possible. Ask them to sit with their mirror for a few minutes and contemplate themselves as a whole package: body, mind, spirit, and soul. Ask them to do this in the spirit of love and acceptance. Enough criticism has already occurred in their lives; this is the time for a moment of self-appreciation.

Words and /or Images about Witness

Ask participants to write or draw their feelings about the interactive witness session and the individual witness session.

You, and You in Relationship

So then, the relationship of self to other is the complete realization that loving yourself is impossible without loving everything defined as other than yourself.

~ ALAN WATTS ~

Aims and Intentions
- Review the importance of your relationship to your true self
- Helena's story

Tools and/or Exercises
- Your hands and healing
- Washing of hands
- Decorating the traced hands

Materials
- Drawing paper and pencils
- Water and bowls
- Art supplies as well as various items from craft store (hearts, buttons, string, glue, glitter, pebbles, sequins, water colors, feathers, pipe cleaners, tissue paper)
- Pens or pencils and paper or journals

Healing your relationship with yourself is an ongoing process. At the personal level, you possess great ability to heal, and it can start with your own two hands.

Touch. It is perhaps the most important element in all relationships. Helena had never been loved, or touched, by another human being.

Helena's Story

In the Greek language, Helena means "bright, shining light." My work with Helena made me realize that some individuals go through life being and feeling unloved, and that the mere act of human touch, much less loving touch, is foreign to them. When we did the rock and flower exercise in which rocks signify hardship and trauma and flowers are moments of love, wellbeing and happiness Helena asked to leave the room.

I stepped out of the room and found her weeping. Helena said that she didn't have a single flower to reflect upon. I asked if I could hold her while she cried and she allowed me to do so.

The act of being touched by another human being, and experiencing the caring and warm touch of another was freeing for her. It touched a place deep within that had gone dark. After that moment, Helena's light could be seen by the other members of our group through the beauty of her smile.

The sorrow we'd seen when she told us that one of her children had committed suicide was replaced by the pride Helena carried into the room the day she announced that her social worker had recommended Helena's youngest daughter be removed from foster care and returned to her.

How does knowing Helena's story influence your perspective on touch?

Loving acts of kindness manifest themselves in different ways, all of which are necessary and useful. The hand held with empathy, a hug of support, a pat on the back for a job well done—gentle, loving touch is a powerful connector and a universal tool of healing.

Your Hands and Healing

You can do this activity individually but if there is a group, it is nice to pair up and share the exercise. One person places their hand, palm down, on the blank paper. The other person takes a pencil and traces the outline of the person's hand. Take your time, be slow, careful, and deliberate while outlining the shape of the hand, and remain silent. When the first hand is outlined, on a second piece of paper do the same with the person's opposite hand. Now switch, so the person whose hands were already outlined draws the partner's hands.

This is a powerful exercise because it involves active witness on the part of each individual. The one who is having the outline of his or her hand traced experiences the sensation of the pencil as it moves around their fingers. The two people are both concentrating thought on the person whose hand is being traced. They are both witnessing and feeling the power and the miracle of the human hand.

Washing of Hands

The second part of this exercise is to return to the person you paired with for the tracing. Each pair is given a warm bowl of water and two paper towels. They each wash the other's hands (no soap, just water) in the same spirit that Jesus demonstrated when He washed the feet of the Apostles. This ritual should be carried out quietly and reverently. It is a gesture of humble service. As your partner rests their hands in the bowl and you gently wash their fingers, thumb, palms, know that you are healing them. This is an exercise when two people get to act in service of one another. When the activity is done, each may assist in drying each other's hands.

Decorating the Traced Hands

Taking all the experiences encountered during the tracing and washing of the hands, you now get to decorate the tracings of your hands with the art supplies and various items. Use your imagination to create a mosaic on the traced outline. As you work, identify feelings about yourself and feelings about your body that the exercises brought into consciousness.

1. What was it like being touched?
2. Was it nurturing?
3. Did it make you uncomfortable? If so, why?
4. What's it like to touch another?

Healing with Humor by Seeking Your Clown

You can discover more about a person in an hour of play than in a year of conversation.

~ PLATO ~

Aims and Intentions
- Work toward self-expression through play, humor, and joy
- Faustino's story

Tools and/or Exercises
- Hold a clown nose prop to get in touch with emotions
- Wear a clown nose as permission to play

Materials
- Clown noses

Here is the "clown" as defined by www.merriam-webster.com: "clown:

noun \ 'klau̇n \ 1 : farmer, countryman 2 : a rude ill-bred person : boor

3 a : a fool, jester, or comedian in an entertainment (such as a play); specifically : a grotesquely dressed comedy performer in a circus b : a person who habitually jokes and plays the buffoon c : joker."

Getting permission to be a clown isn't a matter of learning to do 'funny' things. Rather it consists of discovering the part of self that can be clown-like (silly, funny, fun-loving) and stepping into the freedom of that light behavior.

Clown noses can be ordered in bulk, prices range from 25¢ to 50¢ each; alternatives to the foam noses are inexpensive lipstick, washable paint or double-stick tape and circles of red construction paper.

Although he never finished the program, Faustino's humor will live on in the memory of his classmates. Some stories, even ones with humor, do not have a happy ending.

Faustino's Story

There are those amongst us who have a keen wit and good sense of humor, always ready with a joke or a funny observation. Faustino was that person in our group. He also had a dark side that manifested itself in his struggles with alcohol addiction and the sporadic ability to control the rage hidden behind his humor.

The one thing that always made him smile was his son Faustino, Jr. Every time he was in our group, Faustino shared a story about Junior who was born with cerebral palsy and was wheelchair bound throughout childhood. When Faustino joined our group Junior was 21 and bedridden due to pulmonary problems.

The day after his son died from pulmonary complications, Faustino came to the group because all the men had become honorary godparents to Junior. When we attended the viewing, Faustino was emotionally distraught. More than once I, one of the men, or a family member had to pull him away from the open casket.

A few weeks after Junior's passing we worked on the clown nose exercise and Faustino had us laughing hysterically as he pantomimed bathing and dressing Junior after a bath.

The loss of his son darkened Faustino's life, but humor could offer relief. The loss of human life, and the emotion of grief, is one of the most complicated situations anyone has to face. Grief can be a trap, or a gateway. Let Faustino's story ask you the questions you want to ask yourself about grief.

Hold Your Nose!

People who act as clowns are willing to be vulnerable. They are professional empathizers to their own feelings and those of the audience. The clown is a magician, a transformer of the inner world, and an elevator of the human spirit.

Pass out red clown noses to the group. Ask group members now holding the nose in their hands to close their eyes. Then ask them these questions and let them think through the answers: "What does it feel like?" "Does it have a smell?" "Does it feel good or intimidating?"

Tell them that the clown nose represents hopes, fears, dreams, beliefs, and emotions. The nose is the "now;" the present moment where the only thing that matters is togetherness and play. If holding the nose makes a person feel vulnerable, put other words to it—words such as freedom, cunning, mischief, joy, magic.

Put on the Clown Nose

Ask everyone to bend over, or turn away from the group. Instruct them to place the clown nose over their nose. Don't turn around until the nose is in place and you feel ready. Once the nose is on, treat it with respect. The following is a list of things you can act out once the nose is on. Feel free to make up your own story.

- Pretend you are given a bouquet of flowers by a lover then set down the flowers and walk away, and come back and act as if the lover who'd given you the flowers has just left you

- You've just saved a life and are being presented flowers for being a hero
- Paint your toenails as if you are unsure about how to do it
- Pretend to play a piano with great joy
- You've received an envelope with a gift of $1,000
- Other emotions and attitudes to enact while wearing your nose: puzzled, bored, jealous, lusty, tired, cautious, knowledgeable, worried, angry, confused, arrogant, naughty
- Music is an option if it's too difficult to act out given scenarios; just dance while wearing the clown nose

Lights, Camera, Action, and... Shadow

The Enneagram number you find is not for the sake of mere self-categorization, it is for the enlightenment of the person, by helping them to recognize their own addictive pattern of seeing and thinking.

~ FATHER RICHARD ROHR ~

Aims and Intentions
* Learn to see and live with the quantities of light and shadow in self and others
* Alma's story

Tools and/or Exercises
* Enneagram assessment
* Deep dive into Enneagram
* Words and/or images on the topic of man as machine
* Creating the false self

Materials
* Enneagram lecture: www.youtube.com/watch?v=epl2zOQ2iA4
* Post-it® large tablet and Sharpie® marker
* Pens or pencils and paper or journals

It's time to go backstage, into the shadows of the human psyche. One way to do this is to use the Enneagram tool. One of the people who taught about the Enneagram is a Bolivian philosopher named Oscar Ichazo who founded the

Arica School, now based in the U.S. and known as the Arica Institute (http://www.arica.org/.) He found that the Enneagram (or Enneagon, as he calls the nine-sided figure) organizes the various laws operating in the human person.

Another person credited with use of this tool is George Gurdjieff (1879-1949), a Russian teacher of esoteric knowledge and a contemporary of Freud. Gurdjieff used the Enneagram to explain the laws involved in the creation and unfolding of all the aspects of the universe.

While Gurdjieff applied the Enneagram's process to all of reality, including a rudimentary application to the human person, Ichazo made use of the Enneagram figure and dynamics to explain more fully the functioning of the human psyche.

There was no light or action in Alma's life. She was in a loveless marriage; her children had contempt for her, as she had for them. She had no sense of who she was and how she got to that place.

Alma's Story

Her disdain and hatred for her ex-husband was palpable and at the same time Alma also harbored repressed resentment for her two living sons. Her problems began when she lost her eldest son in a car accident at age 16. She blames herself for the accident because she initially said no when her son asked to borrow the car, but he pestered her until she gave in to his request. Her youngest son was also in the car accident but walked away with minor injuries.

After the accident, the younger son was never the same. To make up for his trauma Alma indulged him in every way. At age 27 he was still living at home, couldn't hold down a job, and was dealing drugs. Alma's middle son was living in Chicago, but she doesn't know where because he'd only contact her when he needed money.

It was clear to everyone in the group that Alma was depressed and struggling with an alcohol addiction. When she came to our group Alma had been sober for three months, but a few weeks into group, she relapsed after a fight with her youngest son. It started when she told him he needed to get his act together or she was going to kick him out of the house. He responded by throwing beer in her face.

Enneagram Assessment

When people are given a chance to see themselves in an objective way, they are able to see the patterns they use to cope with life. Some of these patterns might be the negative, addictive behaviors that result from ACEs. By discovering the 'shadow side' of your personality, in contrast to your 'lights-camera-action' public persona side, you can get a better sense of the importance of taking responsibility for all your behaviors...and get a better sense of how other people view you.

It's been said that because of darkness, we know light. When people become aware of both the dark and the light within themselves, they can live a life of greater purpose, joy, love, and freedom. The contrast between dark and light in a personality is especially visible if observed through the lens of a machine such as a camera or the test result from the Enneagram. If you think of the Enneagram, or the camera, as a "tool," you can imagine a human being like a "machine" that runs on the energies of lightness and darkness.

Father Rohr believes that when one lives right they will enjoy life. That does not mean that there will not be suffering, difficulty, and hardships. Even underneath despair there can be contentment. You become aware of: "I am who I am and it's OK." Goodness and badness, when seen together, blend into a self that includes God, the Source, whatever you chose to call a Higher Power. This is how to use your dark side, your shadow self, to bring you together with God, the Higher Power, itself.

See Father Rohr's Enneagram work on the internet at www.youtube.com/watch?v=epl2zOQ2iA4.

Overview of the Enneagram Types

Type 1: The Need for Perfection (fear of being defective; desire to be good)

Type 2: The Need to Be Needed (fear of being unwanted; desire to be loved)

Type 3: The Need to Succeed (fear of being worthless; desire to be appreciated)

Type 4: The Need to Be Special (fear of being ordinary; desire to stand out)

Type 5: The Need to Perceive (fear of being useless; desire to feel capable)

Type 6: The Need to Be Secure (fear of lack; desire to be supported)

Type 7: The Need to Avoid Pain (fear of being deprived; desire for contentment)

Type 8: The Need to Be Against (fear of being controlled; desire for feeling of freedom)

Type 9: The Need to Avoid (fear of loss; desire for peace of mind)

The Nine Types

Type 1 - The Need to Be Perfect
- Basic Fear - Being corrupt/evil, defective
- Basic Desire - To be good, to have integrity, to be balanced

Type Two - The Need to Be Needed
- Basic Fear - Being unwanted, unworthy of being loved
- Basic Desire - To feel loved

Type Three - The Need to Succeed
- Basic Fear - Being worthless
- Basic Desire - To feel valuable and worthwhile

Type Four – The Need to Be Special
- Basic Fear - Being ordinary
- Basic Desire - Being in balance and at peace

Type Five - The Need to Perceive
- Basic Fear - Being useless, helpless or incapable
- Basic Desire - To be capable and competent

Type Six - The Need for Security
- Basic Fear - Being without support and guidance
- Basic Desire - To have security and support

Type Seven - The Need to Avoid Pain
- Basic Fear - Being deprived and in pain
- Basic Desire - To be satisfied and content—to have their needs fulfilled

Type Eight - The Need to Be Against
- Basic Fear - Being harmed or controlled by others
- Basic Desire - To protect themselves (to be in control of their own life and destiny)

Type Nine - The Need to Avoid
- Basic Fear - Loss and separation
- Basic Desire - To have inner stability, "peace of mind"

Deep Dive into Enneagram

Study the Enneagram types and list characteristics of each. Spend 15 to 20 minutes looking over each type and its attributes and choosing the type that you think best fits. Individually or in a group, write down or have a discussion using the following questions to guide you:

- Why did you pick that specific personality type?
- Do you currently see yourself exhibiting the positive or negative relationship traits of that type?
- How can you begin to work towards conversion and maturation?
- Often we share a number of characteristics of the various types; what might they be?

Words and/or Images on Man as a Machine

George Ivanovich Gurdjieff said, "Man such as we know him, is a machine." Gurdjieff was a Russian-Greco-Armenian mystic. He was an author and a teacher of "The Work," also known as "The Fourth Way." He taught exercises on how to focus one's attention and awareness and believed that spiritual development and evolution could occur in humans who used his methods.

Here are two more quotes from Gurdjieff to consider: "Without self-knowledge, without understanding the working and functions of his machine, man cannot be free, he cannot govern himself and he will always remain a slave." And, "It is the greatest mistake to think that man is always one and the same. A man is never the same for long. He is continually changing. He seldom remains the same even for half an hour."

Creating the False Self

Write, draw, or create a collage of your experience and impressions of the Enneagram, as well as thoughts about the human "machines," self-knowledge, and the changing nature of human beings.

As you write or draw, contemplate the four ways in which we go about creating our false self. This allows you to find clarity about where you currently find yourself.

1. We split from our shadow self and pretend to be our idealized self.

2. We split our mind from our body and soul and live in our minds.

3. We split life from death and try to live our life without any "death."
4. We split ourselves from other selves and try to live apart, superior, and separate.

Your Spiritual Truths

*Lord, make me an instrument of thy peace.
Where there is hatred, let me sow love,
Where there is injury, pardon;
Where there is doubt, faith;
Where there is despair, hope;
Where there is darkness, light;
And where there is sadness, joy.
Grant that we may not seek to be
Consoled as to console; to be understood
As to understand; to be loved as to love.
For it is in giving that we receive; it is in
Pardoning that we are pardoned; and it is in dying that we are
born to eternal life.*

~ SAINT FRANCIS OF ASSISI ~

Aims and Intentions
- Orient to a belief system that serves your highest good
- Constantine's story

Tools and/or Exercises
- Reconnect to Maslow's "Hierarchy of Needs"
- Poem by Hafiz, "Once a Young Woman Said to Me"
- Questions and responses in pairs
- Invitation to what you want to know exercise
- Touching the spirit meditation
- Words and/or images exercise about being present

Materials

- Link to Maslow's "Hierarchy of Needs" https://www.simplypsychology.org/maslow.html
- Link to poem by Hafiz, http://yearwithhafiz.blogspot.com/2013/12/once-young-woman-said-to-me.html
- Link to poem by Oriah: http://www.oriahmountaindreamer.com/
- Link to meditation: www.ignatianspirituality.com/8078/prayer-of-theilhard-de-chardin
- Post-it® large tablet and Sharpie® marker
- Pens or pencils and paper or journals

Jesus, Mohammed, Buddha, Saint Francis, and all masters and soul guides of every spiritual tradition teach that moving from the 'small self' to the 'true self' requires a commitment to an inner journey. For example, Jesus made this point clear through dying on the cross, and Buddha reached enlightenment while remaining on Earth to teach. For both of these spiritual leaders, suffering was integral to self-realization. Self-knowledge is a path that requires suffering that leads to inner work. Self-knowledge in the human being is heart-rending, perilous, challenging, and distressing.

As Ken Wilbur wrote in the preface to the book *Integral Life Practice: A 21st Century Blueprint for Physical Health, Emotional Balance, Mental Clarity, and Spiritual Awakening:* "At the Integral stages of development, the entire universe starts to make sense, to hang together, to actually appear as a uni-verse—a 'one world'—a single, unified, integrated world that unites not only different philosophies and ideas about the world, but different practices for growth and development as well."

Humans develop in a field of experiences followed by feelings. Regarding the measurements involved in this field, Maslow observed that people are motivated to achieve certain needs, some needs take precedence over others, and basic stages of development follow either a straight or winding path. ACEs makes fulfilling needs difficult to access, but not impossible. In order to reach the final stage, which is self-actualization, people must take up some form of contemplative or meditative practice—tools or skills available to all, no matter where you find yourself on the self-actualization pyramid.

An area of misjudgment that has been made regarding those of us who have experienced ACEs is the undue focus on the event or events that engendered the trauma. This error has caused us to see ourselves as victims, perpetrators, or survivors rather than human beings with an instinctual power to heal.

The story Constantine told focuses on individual spiritual truths of trust, faith, and vulnerability as he walks a winding path of self-actualization.

Constantine's Story

Constantine was raised in the United States because his parents left Mexico and crossed the desert into California when he was 5 years old. Constantine (which means "faith") is now 45 years old and doesn't have any ties to Mexico. His wife and five children, the only family he has, are in San Bernardino and he needed to get back to them.

For most of his adult life, Constantine made a living as a house painter in San Bernardino. Lately, due to hard economic times, the work has dried up and his painting business hasn't been going so well. In a sense, that's why he says he ended up in our group. "I was losing my house and got depressed. I started arguing with my wife because of the bills and that's when my neighbor called the cops on me. The cops handed me over to the Migra." (Migra is his term for the immigration authorities).

He got sent back to Mexico, but came back across the border in a way that was illegal. "I got dropped off at a Taco Bell in San Bernardino, and had to pay the coyote $5,000 dollars."

After returning to California, Constantine turned to alcohol. "It's very hard right know but I ain't gonna give up," he said. "I got to keep trying cause I want to be with my family; keep trying no matter what, no matter what it takes."

As he talked, Constantine gently rubbed the Santa Muerte talisman he wore around his neck. It's a female skeleton wearing a hood and holding a scythe like the grim reaper. The scythe and her deathly appearance symbolize her power over life and death.

Many people who have an undocumented immigration status pray to Santa Muerte for protection. When a person is faced with death every day, a new realm opens to spiritual truths in the ways to cope.

Reconnect with Maslow's Hierarchy of Needs

Use the Post-it® large tablet and Sharpie® marker to write out the levels of this scale:

> **Level 1** Physical survival; breathing, food, water, sex, sleep, health.
>
> **Level 2** Safety; access and moral, family, land resources; employment, physical security and physical wellbeing.
>
> **Level 3** Love or belonging; friendship, family, sexual intimacy.
>
> **Level 4** Esteem; achievement, respect of others, respect by others, confidence; small self.
>
> **Level 5** Self-actualization; true self, morality, creativity, flow.

As you list the levels, engage the group in discussion that leads to how the ability to break down suffering in order to write and read poetry exemplifies self-actualization.

Poem by Hafiz, "Once a Young Woman Said to Me"

The man who translated the work of the poet Hafiz keeps this poem nearby because it informs his work. See http://yearwithhafiz.blogspot.ro/2013/12/once-young-woman-said-to-me.html. The importance of this poem is about the knife as a metaphor for human suffering.

Questions and Responses in Pairs

Break into pairs. One person will begin by asking a question of the other. It is more comfortable for the person being asked the question to close their eyes as this will help with focus.

Questioner: What is it that you hope for?

The person responding answers with whatever thought or thoughts come into their mind. When finished, they acknowledge the person asking the question by saying "Thank you."

Allow a moment to let the answer reverberate. When ready, ask the same question again.

Question: What is it that you hope for?

Again, the person responding answers with whatever thought or thoughts come to mind.

This process goes on for three minutes. The questioner asks and the respondent answers. Once the three minutes are up switch; the person who first answered now asks the question, gets the response, is thanked, allows time for the answer to reverberate, then asks the question again.

When each person has both asked and answered, reflect on the following three questions:

1. How hard or easy is it to stay with the responses given?
2. Did you find yourself going into your own thoughts and story?
3. What did you learn from this exercise about your ability to be present for the "other?"

Invitation to What You Want to Know

Staying in pairs, review the poem "The Invitation" by Oriah (http://www.oriahmountaindreamer.com).

With a partner, take turns talking about what you want to know about the other person, and what's unique about you that you want others to know. Listen to the way you use your voice when speaking, and listen to the other person with the same attention.

Touching the Spirit Meditation

Now, each pair sits in silence. Ask them to place their attention on slow, steady, and peaceful breathing.

After a few minutes, recite the words of Pierre Teilhard de Chardin found here: www.ignatianspirituality.com/8078/prayer-of-theilhard-de-chardin. (It is an excerpt from *Hearts on Fire: Praying with Jesuits,* a book by Michael Harter, SJ).

Words and/or Images about Being Present

Either draw or write about the ability to sit and be present. Write or draw what came to you throughout the meditation. Think about what these thoughts and feelings mean in response to the belief systems that you've carried—the ones that are perhaps lodged in your subconscious. Ask and answer whether those thoughts and belief systems are rational, logical, good for health, and in your best interests.

Past, Present, Hope, Healing

Wisdom begins in wonder.

~ SOCRATES ~

Aims and Intentions
- Let go of the small self and shadow; meet your true self
- James's story

Tools and/or Exercises
- Review Rilke's poem, "I Believe in All that Has Never Yet Been Spoken"
- Forgiveness meditation
- Drumming exercise
- Burning ceremony

Materials
- Link to poem by Rilke: http://www.poetry-chaikhana.com/blog/2011/01/14/rainer-maria-rilke-i-believe-in-all-that-has-never-yet-been-spoken/
- Drums or anything that can be used as a percussion instrument
- Link to drumming information: https://www.youtube.com/watch?v=tYt3WJZsW_M
- Pens or pencils and paper or journals

There is a wonderful story of a young seeker who, keen to become the student of a certain master, was invited to an interview at the master's house. The student rambled on about all his spiritual experience, his past teachers, his insights and skills, and his pet philosophies. The master listened silently and poured a cup of tea. He poured and poured and when the cup overflowed, he kept right on pouring. Eventually the student noticed the flood of tea and interrupted his monologue to say, "Stop pouring! The cup is full."

The teacher replied, "Yes, and so are you. How can I possibly teach you?"

If you are to achieve peace and harmony in your life, and in the lives of others, you must begin by working from the outside in. Be willing to surrender to the mystery. Understand that we are all one. The South African concept of Ubuntu preached by Anglican archbishop and human rights activist Desmond Tutu expresses this sentiment beautifully: Ubuntu—my humanity is intertwined with yours. I "am" because you "are." I cannot be sated, if you are hungry. I can't be rich, while you are poor. I can't be safe, while you are in danger. I can't be happy, while you are in pain.

Every single story is interconnected in some way. Martin Luther King, Jr. wrote "Letter from Birmingham Jail" on April 16, 1963 to say to every reader: "In a real sense all life is inter-related. All men are caught in an inescapable network of mutuality, tied in a single garment of destiny. Whatever affects one directly, affects all indirectly. I can never be what I ought to be until you are what you ought to be, and you can never be what you ought to be until I am what I ought to be...."

We are all on a journey—a hero's journey. Every story has a beginning, a middle, and an end.

In the world of science, the experimenter is always involved in the experiment. In the world of books, the author is an integral part of the manuscript. Here, I am taking the liberty to share the story of my father and myself. At a significant moment in my life with my father, I asked him, "Why can't you just love me?" and neither of us had the answer. I know the answer now…it was because he never felt loved. At the end of his life, we both experienced a measure of healing.

James's Story

In May 2017, I packed everything I had into my Toyota RAV4 and drove across the country to care for my dying father, the same man I tried to kill some 34 years earlier.

Prior to making that journey, I read the book, Gandhi the Man: The Story of His Transformation, *by Eknath Easwaran. At one point in in his life, Gandhi was asked to tell in three words what he understands to be the secret to life. He answered, "Renounce and enjoy!"*

Here, in Gandhi's own words from that book (on page 105), is what this concept meant to him: "By detachment I mean that you must not worry whether the desired results follow from your actions or not, so long as your motive is pure, your means correct. Really it means that things will come right in the end if you take care of the means and leave the rest to Him."

The two months I cared for my father was not an easy time, but it was filled with grace. Grace has many definitions, according to www.merriam-webster.com. "grace: noun \ 'grās \ 1 a : unmerited divine assistance given to humans for their regeneration or sanctification b : a virtue coming from God c : a state of sanctification enjoyed through divine assistance

2 a : approval, favor stayed in his good graces *b archaic : mercy, pardon*

c : a special favor : privilege each in his place, by right, not grace, shall rule his heritage *—Rudyard Kipling d : disposition to or an act or instance of kindness, courtesy, or clemency e : a temporary exemption : reprieve*

3 a : a charming or attractive trait or characteristic Among disagreeable qualities he possessed the saving grace of humor *b : a pleasing appearance or effect : charm* all the grace of youth *—John Buchan c : ease and suppleness of movement or bearing* danced with such grace

4 used as a title of address or reference for a duke, a duchess, or an archbishop

5 a short prayer at a meal asking a blessing or giving thanks

6 Graces plural : three sister goddesses in Greek mythology who are the givers of charm and beauty

7 : a musical trill, turn, or appoggiatura

8 a : sense of propriety or right had the grace not to run for elective office *—Calvin Trillin b : the quality or state of being considerate or thoughtful* accepted his advice with grace."

In the evenings, prior to sharing the food I cooked, we took turns saying grace, always clinking our wine-filled glasses and saying "salud" before having our first taste. When I bathed him in the mornings, every so often I was overcome with a sense of wonder, humility, and gratitude. The few times I was there to clean up a mess, change his clothes, or lift him up were gifts—and now memories—that have left me with a sense of wonder, possibility, and hope.

Poem by Rainer Maria Rilke: "I Believe in All that Has Never Yet Been Spoken"

In the large group, read the poem from http://www.poetry-chaikhana.com/blog/2011/01/14/rainer-maria-rilke-i-believe-in-all-that-has-never-yet-been-spoken/. During the first reading, ask people in your group to listen with their hearts for a phrase or word that resonates.

In the second reading, reflect on what touches the heart, and allow people to speak their responses aloud.

Read the passage a third time and ask the participants to reach an understanding of what the poem is calling them to do.

To make this point hit home, consider a short, ecumenical prayer by an anonymous poet:

Thank you for giving me good work to do.

Thank you for showing me how to do it.

Thank you for giving me a good life to live.

Thank you for showing me how to live it.

Thank you for giving me people to love.

Thank you for showing me how best to love them.

Forgiveness Meditation

This "forgiveness meditation" is a way of opening to the possibilities of true healing and love for self and others. It produces a soft, gentle, and loving way to accept whatever arises and to leave it be, without trying to control it with either actions or thoughts.

Let yourself sit comfortably, close your eyes; breathe in a natural, easy pattern. Relax body, mind, and spirit. Sense your heart's location and beat, and let yourself feel all the barriers you have erected, the emotions that you carry because you have not forgiven yourself or others. Feel the pain of keeping your heart closed. While breathing in a quiet, deep way, ask for and extend forgiveness. Let images and feelings that come up as you are guided; feel them grow deeper.

General Forgiveness: "There are many ways that I have hurt and harmed myself and others. I have betrayed or abandoned myself many times through thought, word or deed, knowingly or unknowingly."

Let yourself see the ways you have hurt or harmed yourself and others; picture the moments, events, experiences; remember them. Feel the feelings you have carried from this and sense that you can release these burdens. Extend forgiveness for each of them, one by one.

Self-Forgiveness: "For the ways I have hurt myself through action or inaction, out of fear, pain and confusion, I now extend a full and heartfelt forgiveness. I forgive myself. I forgive myself. I forgive myself."

Asking for Full Forgiveness: "There are many ways that I have hurt and harmed myself and others, have betrayed or abandoned them or myself, causing suffering, knowingly or unknowingly, out of my pain, fear, anger and confusion."

Let yourself remember and visualize the ways you have hurt yourself and others. See and feel the pain you have caused out of your own fear and confusion. Feel your own sorrow and regret as you feel theirs, too. Sense that finally you can release this burden and ask for full forgiveness. Picture each memory that still burdens your heart. Then, to each person in your mind, repeat: "I ask for your forgiveness, I ask for your forgiveness."

Forgiving Those Who Have Hurt You: "There are many ways that I have been harmed by others, abused or abandoned, knowingly or unknowingly, in thought, word or deed."

Let yourself picture and remember these many ways. Feel the sorrow you have carried from this past. Feel, know, and sense that you can release this burden of pain by extending forgiveness when your heart is ready.

Now say to yourself: "I now remember the many ways others have hurt, harmed me or wounded me, out of fear, pain, confusion and anger. I have carried this pain in my heart too long. To the extent that I am ready, I offer them forgiveness. To those who have caused me harm, I offer my forgiveness. I forgive you. I forgive you. I forgive you."

Let yourself gently repeat these meditations for forgiveness until you feel a release in your heart. For some great pains, you may not feel a release but only the burden, anguish, or anger you have held. Touch this softly; be kind to it. Be forgiving of yourself for not being ready to let go and move on.

Forgiveness cannot be forced; it cannot be artificial. Continue to practice and let the words and images work gradually in their own way. In time, with this forgiveness meditation as a regular part of your life, you will be able to let go of the past, the memories, and open your heart to each new moment with a wisdom, and loving kindness.

Drumming and *Ho'oponopono* Prayer

Drumming in community or alone, people share their spirits in the form of rhythm. It changes relationships for the positive. You can experience the power of drumming if you go to Christine Stevens' YouTube channel: https://www.youtube.com/user/ubdrumcircles.

Playing drums alone and together, you give permission to transcend the space and allow for emotional release and healing. There is no right or wrong way to drum other than allowing your own sense of rhythm to guide you. When you are in a drumming circle, know that the release and healing is different for every person in the circle. A sense of satisfaction will happen whether drumming in the circle, or standing outside and simply bringing your willingness to the circle.

The act of drumming involves several physical senses. In his "Daily Meditation" newsletter, Father Richard Rohr shared a quote from John O'Donohue: "Your mind can deceive you and put all kinds of barriers between you and your nature; but your body does not lie."

Allow the drumming to take over and to end organically, when the time feels right.

When the drumming has ended rest in silence for three to five minutes.

When the silence ends, hand out pencils or pens and paper. Ask group members to write the name of a person they are ready to forgive, or with whom they wish to begin a journey of forgiveness. Once the name is written, have them fold the paper and drop it into a sturdy, heat resistant urn or bowl. Place the urn or bowl in the center of the circle; have members stand and join hands. When the all papers have all been deposited, set a flame to them. As they burn away, speak forgiveness in the ancient Hawaiian practice of *Ho'oponopono* until the fire has dissipated and all papers have burned. Here is the *ho'oponopono* prayer:

I'm Sorry

Please Forgive Me

Thank You

I Love You

Repeat the phrases until papers have all burned. When each member of the group has finished the four phrases and all are present in the moment, the ritual is complete. End with a chosen piece of music ("Amazing Grace," "This Little Light of Mine" or William Blake's poem, "Eternity," below.)

Eternity

He who binds to himself a joy
Does the winged life destroy
He who kisses the joy as it flies
Lives in eternity's sunrise

~ WILLIAM BLAKE ~

www.ingramcontent.com/pod-product-compliance
Lightning Source LLC
Chambersburg PA
CBHW081334080526
44588CB00017B/2618